Psychoanalytic F

M000221569

Written by one of the world's renowned Bionian Field Theory scholars, this foundational volume provides a thorough introduction to all facets of psychoanalytic field theory, one of the most lively and original currents of thought in contemporary psychoanalysis, to offer new answers to age-old questions around how psychic change occurs.

With clinical examples to illuminate key themes of therapeutic effectiveness, current controversies, and future developments, the book presents a radically intersubjective view of the analytic process that focuses on the plane of unconscious communication common to both analyst and patient, moving beyond the I/you division to access the shared substance of the psyche. It centres the unconscious not as a hellish region of the psyche but as an important function of the personality that gives meaning to emotional experience.

Offering clear expositions of complex concepts and linking to more detailed sources of information, this book is important reading for all clinicians, trainees, and students interested in contemporary psychoanalysis.

Giuseppe Civitarese, MD, PhD, is a training and supervising analyst (SPI, APsaA, IPA). He lives in Pavia, Italy. His books include *The Intimate Room: Theory and Technique of the Analytic Field; The Violence of Emotions: Bion and Post-Bionian Psychoanalysis; Truth and the Unconscious*; and *Sublime Subjects: Aesthetic Experience and Intersubjectivity in Psychoanalysis*.

Routledge Introductions to Contemporary Psychoanalysis

Aner Govrin, Ph.D.
Series Editor
Tair Caspi, Ph.D.
Executive Editor
Yael Peri Herzovich
Assistant Editor

"Routledge Introductions to Contemporary Psychoanalysis" is one of the prominent psychoanalytic publishing ventures of our day. It will comprise dozens of books that will serve as concise introductions dedicated to influential concepts, theories, leading figures, and techniques in psychoanalysis covering every important aspect of psychoanalysis.

The length of each book is fixed at 40,000 words.

The series' books are designed to be easily accessible to provide informative answers in various areas of psychoanalytic thought. Each book will provide updated ideas on topics relevant to contemporary psychoanalysis – from the unconscious and dreams, projective identification and eating disorders, through neuropsychoanalysis, colonialism, and spiritual-sensitive psychoanalysis. Books will also be dedicated to prominent figures in the field, such as Melanie Klein, Jacques Lacan, Sandor Ferenczi, Otto Kernberg, and Michael Eigen.

Not serving solely as an introduction for beginners, the purpose of the series is to offer compendiums of information on particular topics within different psychoanalytic schools. We ask authors to review a topic but also address the readers with their own personal views and contribution to the specific chosen field. Books will make intricate ideas comprehensible without compromising their complexity.

We aim to make contemporary psychoanalysis more accessible to both clinicians and the general educated public.

Psychoanalysis and Colonialism: A Contemporary Introduction
Sally Swartz

Psychoanalytic Field Theory: A Contemporary Introduction
Giuseppe Civitarese

Eating Disorders: A Contemporary Introduction
Tom Wooldridge

Psychoanalytic Field Theory

A Contemporary Introduction

Giuseppe Civitarese

Routledge
Taylor & Francis Group

LONDON AND NEW YORK

First published 2023
by Routledge
4 Park Square, Milton Park, Abingdon, Oxon OX14 4RN

and by Routledge
605 Third Avenue, New York, NY 10158

Routledge is an imprint of the Taylor & Francis Group, an informa business

British Library Cataloguing-in-Publication Data
A catalogue record for this book is available from the British Library

Library of Congress Cataloging-in-Publication Data
A catalog record has been requested for this book

ISBN: 978-1-032-11452-1 (hbk)
ISBN: 978-1-032-11451-4 (pbk)
ISBN: 978-1-003-21997-2 (ebk)

DOI: 10.4324/9781003219972

Typeset in Times New Roman
by Taylor & Francis Books

Contents

Introduction

I would like to start immediately by saying that I will not distinguish Bion from Post-Bionian Analytic Field Theory (BFT), especially in relation to its theoretical part. BFT is the most original development of Bion's thought and makes it of great use on the level of treatment technique thanks to grafts taken from other traditions. In part they overlap, even though in actual fact my reading of Bion is inevitably influenced by BFT; at the same time, I hope that the other theoretical roots of BFT will gradually become clearer.

While lying on a continuum that includes classical and Kleinian psychoanalysis, quite a few of Bion's concepts in fact represent a paradigm shift, as described by Kuhn (1962). A completely new vocabulary is introduced, including in particular the notions of transformation and invariance, O, container–contained, grid, hallucinosis, at-one-ment, reverie, negative capability and faith, selected fact, waking dream thought, alpha function, beta and alpha elements, dream thoughts, Language of Achievement, pre-conception, basic assumption, non-psychotic part of the personality, messianic idea, Establishment, etc.

The concept of projective identification is also used in an idiosyncratic sense, to denote not a pathological phenomenon but a physiological means of communication. In the context of a psychoanalysis based on an essentially one-person psychology, projective identification does not yet appear as a truly relational concept. If, however, it is accommodated within a two-person psychology rather than a psychology of the subject seen in isolation, it immediately proves valuable as a way of conferring clinical and technical substance on the concepts of field and proto-mental system.[1] In its strongly relational sense as a mode of unconscious communication that also entails actual interpersonal pressure, projective identification facilitates understanding of the ways and means whereby this shared unconscious area can be formed, and how the actual processes of interindividual influencing can take place.

Nor is that all. Bion overturns the traditional conception of the unconscious and dreams. Dreams are no longer the royal road to the unconscious. Instead, dreaming *creates* the unconscious; "dreaming" here being understood as the ability to assign a personal meaning to experience (or, if you will, to create symbols), which is acquired from the mother at birth. The unconscious becomes a psychoanalytic *function* of the personality. The identification of the unconscious with sociality, with the symbolic, and with both verbal and non-verbal language – with everything that underlies the attainment of subjecthood and the specifically human capacity to think thoughts – is perhaps nowhere clearer than in Bion. There can be no confusion with the unconscious that is of interest to the neurosciences, although, of course, the discoveries made in these fields must be taken into account by psychoanalytic theory.

According to BFT, patient and analyst give life to intersubjective fields. As noted by Ogden (2009), when a patient enters analysis, he in effect *loses his mind*, or, in other words, he sets foot in an intermediate psychological area, or one shared with the analyst. The patient sets up a communication that, because it involves him at such a deep level, can be channelled so as to repair dysfunctional areas in his internal group structure and also to reinstate the ongoing conversation between the various parts of his mind in their constant search for better ways of "thinking" (here unconscious thought, dreaming, thinking, etc., are to be seen as virtually synonymous) about the emotional problem of the moment. For this reason, the use of the classical concepts of transference and countertransference to denote the characteristics of the analytic field may be misleading, since they presuppose a situation in which analysand and analyst confront each other "face to face" as two positive, pure, complete, and separate subjectivities, each somehow "external" to the other. The relational perspective looks to the profiles in Rubin's famous ambiguous figure; BFT looks to the vase.

Incidentally, the ability to move from one perspective to another of a bi-stable figure also explains why there are some repetitions in the book. This depends, on the one hand, on the fact that, as I know from experience, some theoretical issues are a bit difficult to grasp; on the other, because it is important to see the same thing but from different points of view in order to attain a more integrated vision.

Note

1 To explain why individuals have such a strong tendency to link together with each other, Bion postulates the existence of a 'proto-mental system'. This must obviously be thought of as a totality within which individuals are merely dynamic elements in relation to all the others. *All* basic assumptions ("mental activities that have in common the attribute of powerful emotional drives" (Bion, 1961, p. 146), 'the "cement" that keeps the group assembled' (López-Corvo, 2002, p. 39), are considered to have been deposited within this totality even if they are inactive. For Bion too, therefore, the subject is not conceivable apart from its intrinsic social dimension. An individual's psyche transcends the physical limits of that individual; it is *transindividual*. Furthermore, within this system there is no distinction between the bodily and the mental realms.

Chapter I

The origins of field theory

The term "field" is one we can find already in Bion. For instance, in a letter to Rickman dated March 7, 1943, he writes: "The more I look at it the more it seems to me that some very serious work needs to be done along analytical and field theory lines to elucidate... the present system..." (Conci, 2011, p. 82). What is unequivocally a field theory can then be found in the paper, published in *The Lancet* that same year (Bion and Rickman, 1943), and written jointly by both, entitled "Intra-group Tensions in Therapy: Their Study as the Task of the Group", which Lacan (1947) described unhesitatingly as a "miracle". This was to become the first chapter of *Experiences in Groups* (Bion, 1961). However, it was Madeleine and Willy Baranger who were the first to use the concept of field as the basis of a thoroughly new model in psychoanalysis. In their paper "The Analytic Situation as a Dynamic Field", originally published in Spanish in 1961–2, they focus on the unconscious couple-related resistances that impede the analytic process – the so-called bastions. Overcoming these resistances is in their view one of the main aims of analysis. Implicit in this model is the notion that the analyst participates in the relationship with all her subjectivity, that she is inevitably caught up in interactive sequences with the patient, and may appreciate their unconscious meaning only at a later stage.

Normally, when the talk is of BFT, the names of Willy and Madeleine Baranger, and Antonino Ferro come to mind: specifically, the 1961–2 essay by the Barangers, "The Analytic Situation as a

DOI: 10.4324/9781003219972-1

Dynamic Field", and the latter's 1992 book *The Bi-Personal Field: Experiences in Child Analysis.* Between these two texts, in 1990, the book *La situazione psicoanalitica come campo bipersonale* (The Psychoanalytic Situation as a Bipersonal Field) by Baranger and Baranger was published in Italy, edited by Antonino Ferro and Stefania Manfredi, both analysts who were members of the Italian Psychoanalytic Society and the International Psychoanalytic Association. As we can see, the book takes up the title of the essay of thirty years earlier, but also introduces other essays. It is interesting to bear in mind that this article was translated into French for the first time in 1985, into English only in 2008 and into German in 2018. We need to wait until 2009, however, to find a volume in English by the two Argentine authors: edited by Leticia Glocer, *The Work of Confluence: Listening and Interpreting in the Psychoanalytic Field*, contains ten of their articles. In the book there are a mere three references to Bion. The only really significant reference is in the passage where the authors admit (but only in the 1993 essay that forms the fifth chapter) that their concept of the basic phantasy of the analytic couple has its origin not only in Melanie Klein's concept of unconscious phantasy but also in the concept of basic assumptions in groups, as described by Bion (1961) – in other words, a phantasy that does not exist in either participant outside of the group situation.

Although the Barangers do not quote Bion in their now classic paper, Madeleine Baranger (Churcher, 2008) later acknowledged that she had been influenced by him ever since the early 1950s:

> It was when we reviewed Bion's studies on small groups that we modified and added precision to our thinking in a direction different from transference–countertransference interaction [...]. We then understood that the field is much more than interaction and intersubjective relations [...]. Translating what is described as the group's "basic assumption" to the individual analytic situation, we spoke of the "basic unconscious phantasy" that emerges in the analytic situation, created by the same field situation [...]. This phantasy is not the sum or combination of the individual fantasies of the two members of the analytic couple, but an original set of fantasies created by the field situation itself. It emerges in the process of the

analytic situation and has no existence outside the field situation, although it is rooted in the unconscious of the members.
(Baranger, 2005, p. 62f.)

The Barangers are cited a total of 1,656 times in PEP: 284 times before 1990, and 1,383 times after that date. To understand the "Ferro-effect" on the popularity of the Barangers, we need only consider that in the five-year period 1985–1989, 12 out of 46 citations are by Italian authors, in the two-year period 1990–1991, 11 out of 22, and in the two-year period 1992–1993, 29 out of 58. Among them, besides Ferro and Manfredi, we find Adolfo Pazzagli, Gregorio Hautmann, Luciana Nissim Momigliano, Fernando Riolo, Basilio Bonfiglio, Michele Bezoari, Francesco Barale and Cono Barnà. All of this shows how the reception of the Barangers' ideas in Italy, three decades after the publication of their seminal paper, now the most quoted in the whole of psychoanalytic literature, and the grafting of these ideas onto Bion's, contributed enormously to their fame.

But the article which definitively established a clear link between the contributions of the Barangers and Bion came out some years later and was written by Bezoari and Ferro (1989). As far as I have been able to reconstruct, this article, "Listening, Interpretations and Transformative Functions in the Analytical Dialogue", published in the same year in both Italian and English, marks the birth of BFT.

Among the authors who then entered into the synthesis developed initially by Bezoari and Ferro and later carried forward especially by the latter and some of his followers, in addition to the Baranger and Bion, we must also mention Josè Bleger. Ferro has always set great store by Bleger's fundamental study (1967) of the "institutional" nature of the setting and of the various components of the individual's so-called *meta-ego* (Civitarese, 2008). Then we have Francesco Corrao, Eugenio Gaburri, Claudio Neri and Robert Langs. By inviting Bion, in the 1970s, to hold seminars at the psychoanalytic centre in Rome, Corrao was the person who promoted his thinking; and in the two-year period 1986–1987 he wrote both on the concept of hermeneutic field, and on narrative as a psychoanalytic category (1986, 1987a, 1987b). In the same two-year period Gaburri published two influential essays on narration and interpretation. Already in 1981, Neri, together with

Corrao, had edited an issue of the *Rivista di Psicoanalisi*, the official journal of the Italian Psychoanalytic Society (SPI or Società psicoanalitica italiana), entirely dedicated to Bion, including articles by Eugenio Gaddini, Mauro Mancia and Ignacio Matte-Blanco. A few years later, together with Antonello Correale and Paola Fadda, he edited *Letture bioniane* (1987). Lastly, to Langs goes the credit for being the first to champion the Barangers' concept of field outside the South American area as early as 1976 in his book entitled *The Bipersonal Field*, whose title he admits he borrowed from their now classic essay. Later, in 1978, Langs published *Interventions in the Bipersonal Field*. In this volume in essence, the American author elucidates his conception of a spiral movement in the analytic dialogue in which immediate unconscious resonances to what has been said are registered.

As we can see, multiple and complex influences converge in BFT. Their synthesis, however, can be seen as the work of Bezoari and Ferro. Over the following thirty years, this development was carried forward mainly by Ferro and the group of students around him that had come together in Pavia from different parts of the country. They had been drawn to Pavia as the seat of a renowned Faculty of Medicine and a School of Psychiatry whose principal teachers were psychoanalysts (Dario De Martis and Fausto Petrella). The names are those found on the covers of various books written together (Ferro et al., 2007) or edited by Ferro (2013, 2016), over a decade. In addition to the present writer, and to limit myself to his narrowest circle of colleagues: Maurizio Collovà, Giovanni Foresti, Fulvio Mazzacane, Elena Molinari, and Pierluigi Politi were later joined by Mauro Manica and Violet Pietrantonio. I should also mention Sara Boffito and David Ventura, from Italy, and from outside Italy, Montana Katz, plus Howard Levine and Lawrence Brown, Jack Fohel and their group; and also Robert Snell and Kelly Fuery.

We can therefore legitimately speak of the Pavia School of Psychoanalysis. The influence exerted by this school has been growing over time. Authoritatively, Kernberg (2011), Elliott and Prager (2016) and Seligman (2017), have listed BFT among the main currents of contemporary psychoanalysis. Kernberg (p. 634) finds that "The most significant overall developments within the contemporary spectrum of psychoanalytic theory […] involve the neo-

Bionian approach, on the one hand, and the relational approach, on the other [...] the neo-Bionian approach has expanded its influence throughout Europe, particularly in Italy, and, to some extent, also in Latin America. under the influence of Ferro's [...] work". Seligman (2017) has drawn up a fascinating map in which he actually identifies five main psychoanalytic orientations: contemporary Kleinians, contemporary Freudians, BFT, relational psychoanalysis and French psychoanalysis.

Let us now try to take a unified view of the history of psychoanalysis and place BFT in this more general framework. If we look at the history of psychoanalysis, we see that it starts with Freud's (1895) *Project for a Scientific Psychology* and has now reached the psychoanalysis of relationship and the psychoanalysis of the analytic field. What does this mean? In the beginning, the perspective is that of a natural science of the psyche, along the lines of chemistry and physics. The analyst puts the patient, his history and his psyche under a lens and thinks he can heal him by explaining the unconscious mechanisms of thought that prompt him to do certain things unwittingly. Over time Freud realizes that as a purely cognitive operation this method does not work. He begins to understand that you have to go through the experience of the therapeutic relationship. This is configured as a new kind of "experimental" neurosis, on the model of the infantile neurosis – but this time "with the analyst in it".

The analyst acts as a *blank screen* onto which the patient projects the unconscious images of his parents. However, as we can see, the analyst must still come into play. Step by step, analysts realize that they also have a transference and a counter-transference. With Melanie Klein, the analyst's involvement grows further. By means of *projective identification*, the patient has the unconscious phantasy that he can control the analyst from within and not only project *onto* her. A further step is taken with the development of the concept of *enactment*. A split-off part of the patient repeats long-standing relational patterns, and in some way manages to involve the analyst as a character in the drama being played out in analysis, but more or less without her knowledge. Then come the various concepts of "third" or "thirdness", which to varying degrees postulate that from the encounter between minds a *third, shared* mind is formed that obeys its own laws.

These versions of "third", with enactment as a possible variant, are, all in all, still circumscribed. Furthermore, the purpose of analysis is still to reconstruct the patient's history and the traumas he has suffered through the investigation of how the relationship is influenced by these phenomena, or else to reintegrate a split-off part of his personality whose nature is defined precisely by these biographical elements.

Clearly, the common thread that links the whole succession of psychoanalytic models over time lies in the attempt to give a more accurate account of how the analyst (her personality, her unconscious) contributes to the facts of the analysis. The extreme extension of this tendency is Bion's psychoanalysis and its subsequent development as embodied in BFT. Why is this so? Because in my opinion there is no other theory that in such a radical and rigorous way prescribes that the analyst should put aside past and concrete reality and focus as much as possible on the "dream" of the session – where the reference to the dream serves only as a reminder that the analyst must always ask the questions: *Why this? Why now? What does it mean from the perspective of the unconscious?*

This is merely a descriptive proposition; it does not automatically imply a value judgement. It is like saying that potentially, in a session, no matter what they are talking about, either verbally or non-verbally, the analytic couple is always engaged on the unconscious level, like a third mind or dynamic Gestalt or group-of-two, in thinking about itself; that is to say, above all it is trying to give meaning to the experience lived together in the here and now. Just as we need at all times to supply the blood with oxygen through breathing, so we need to supply the mind with meaning.

To put it another way: to expand our mind, we need to constantly create new structures of meaning in the same way as we put LEGO bricks together. The *beta elements*, which is what Bion calls the raw sensations and emotions that affect the body, are like LEGO bricks that lack the little studs that allow them to interlock and thus make it impossible to create new stable objects.

On the unconscious plane, BFT postulates that any communicative exchange is the product of perfect *symmetry*. The analyst comes back to the plane of *asymmetry* when she consciously uses the theories of psychoanalysis to grasp what is happening on the unconscious/symmetric plane of the relationship. Of course, it is not that unconscious communication can be suspended: each wave sets in motion another wave (or cycle). If we accept this reconstruction, we see that there is a surprising continuity in the history of psychoanalysis, however distant Bion and BFT may seem from Freud. Finally, Freud's statement (1921, p. 69) that "from the very first individual psychology [...] is at the same time social psychology as well" assumes effective theoretical form.

The centrality of the concept of field becomes clear. The roots of this concept are ultimately to be traced back to physics. In physics the concept of "field" describes the mutual interdependence and influences at a distance that occur between elements of a given system; later, we find it in Gestalt theory, as well as in the work of Kurt Lewin and in the philosophy of Merleau-Ponty (Bazzi, 2022). The underlying idea is that certain phenomena can only be studied in their dynamic totality, which is considered to be more than the sum of its parts. Furthermore, it is postulated that the investigation of the human mind requires a psychology of the subject in relation to the object. In the 1960s, a few important authors came to the same conclusion: Winnicott noted that the child has no existence (unless it is seen as part of the mother/child dyad/system); Bion, profoundly influenced by his first analyst, John Rickman, argued that the essential thing is to see the analyst/patient couple as a group; from a different perspective, Lacan stressed the radically intersubjective nature of the Ego and the fact that the initial realization of subjectivity stems from the primordial alienation of the subject who sees himself reflected in the object.

We can give Bion the credit for having first introduced, in 1943, the concept of field in psychoanalysis as drawn from physics. Bion points out that "the individual in a group is profiting by his experience if at one and the same time he becomes more accurate in his appreciation of his position in the emotional field, and more capable of accepting it as a fact that even his increased accuracy falls lamentably short of his needs" (1961, p. 45). If the group is more than the sum of the individuals that comprise it, it makes no sense to, as it were, (only) attend to the individuals. *It makes more sense to re-establish in the group the climatic conditions that are conducive to the joint development of the group and the subject.* If, when two individuals come into contact, they are influenced by the emotional field that is generated, there is no point in acting as if it did not exist. Relationship *is* the main therapeutic factor, but then we need to direct our attention not only at what takes place on the *piano nobile* of conscious interaction between the two subjects; we also need to look at what happens on the intersubjective (indistinct) level of the cellar.

Bion's own reference to the concept of field in physics is very specific (and here, obviously, he is talking about individual psychoanalysis):

> According to Heisenberg, in atomic physics a situation has arisen in which the scientist cannot rely on the ordinarily accepted view that the researcher has access to facts, because the facts to be observed are distorted by the very act of observation. Furthermore, the *field* in which he has to observe the relationship of one phenomenon to another is unlimited in extent, and yet none of the phenomena "in" that *field* can be ignored because all interact.
>
> (1965, p. 45, emphasis added)

And further: "A patient who, in my view, is displaying projective transformation and requires the use of Kleinian theories for comprehension, also uses a *field* which is not simply the analyst, or his own personality, or even the relationship between himself and the analyst, but all those and *more*" (ibid., p. 114, emphasis added).

I think that in order to understand "late" Bion, that is, his production from *Learning from Experience* (1962a) onwards, his most difficult and controversial writings, and consequently also BFT, it is worth re-reading not only his wonderful essays of the Kleinian period collected in *Second Thoughts* (1967), but also *Experiences in Groups* (1961). Bion spent his life as a scholar – probably without even being fully aware of it, since he hardly ever talks[1] about it – transposing his theory of groups into his theory of individual psychoanalysis. He himself revolutionizes theory but still works as a Kleinian. Despite his brilliant suggestions, he does not fully develop a new technique. To have a toolbox that anyone can use, we have to wait for BFT. In this model, the analyst sees in the analytic pair not two interacting isolated subjects, but a group. There is no "fact" of analysis that cannot be heard as unconsciously co-created, as a group or field phenomenon. It is as in quantum physics: particles are not discrete elements but only vibrations that propagate in the field. Their position is only probabilistic, in the same way, by analogy, as are different interpretations of the same fact.

Note

1 As far as I know, he uses the concept of basic assumption in reference to the individual only once, in *Attention and Interpretation*: "The individual is similarly affected by the *group* emotional situation" (1970, p. 4).

Chapter 2

Basic concepts

The unconscious as a psychoanalytic function of the personality

It is impossible to understand Bion and BFT if we are not aware that the basic postulate from which everything springs is a concept of the unconscious different from that of Freud: the unconscious as a psychoanalytic function of the personality (an expression that seems to be modelled on the Kantian faculty of productive imagination [*produktive Einbildungskraft*]). In other words, a cognitive faculty of the mind is *a priori* to thought, not innate but acquired. *A priori* should not be confused with innate. If the identity of the subject is defined by the possibility of sensing time, of bringing together an infinite series of "nows", there must be an underlying feeling of self. This feeling must be absorbed and developed by the other, that is to say, by the object that provides the child with primary care, since, beyond material care, it necessarily requires the acquisition of language.

The child is born with a "rudimentary consciousness" (Bion, 1967, p. 116). He feels stimuli but he is not conscious of himself. He perceives without understanding. This consciousness, Bion notes, "is not associated with an unconscious". That is to say, all sensory impressions referring to the Self fall into the same category; all are conscious. The receptor organ of this mass of sensory data about the Self gathered by the newborn by means of his "conscious" is the mother's capacity for reverie. It is a wonderful

DOI: 10.4324/9781003219972-2

image: at the dawn of life, the child has the mother (or caregiver) as his unconscious, and thus as a complement to his primitive consciousness! Through her reverie, the ability to receive and transform the child's projective identifications, the mother expresses her love for the child, contains his anxieties, and gives him the means to form his own alpha function and thinking faculty. Bion's concept of the unconscious is largely identical with that of the alpha function of the mind, an expression he adopts to circumvent the problem we have in defining its contours more clearly, and instead enables us to focus on what we more or less know, in other words, on what it *does*. The alpha function is thus a psychic activity that unites different perceptions. It is a function of formatting/ordering the "sensible" experience which lies between the passivity/receptivity of the senses and the activity/spontaneity of the intellect. Then, thanks to the "apparatus for thinking" thoughts, concepts become synthesized. This activity is also present in the dream, where concepts of things are used and, through processes of condensation and displacement — corresponding, as Lacan argued, to the figures of speech of metaphor and metonymy, respectively — new syntheses are created between different representations and dream thoughts.

Bion rejects, or rather reinvents, Freud's primary/secondary process dichotomy (which is why I sometimes write the word as un/conscious, namely, to give an idea of the continuity between conscious and unconscious, like the two sides of a Möbius strip) – as do the neurosciences (Westen, 1999). The binary opposition should perhaps be reformulated as a continuum between, on the one hand, the infinite and uncontrollable production of meaning that occurs in the verbal signifiers of language and in the non-verbal language of images, and on the other, the finiteness of the concept and semantic or verbal meaning. Obviously, each pole of the somato-psychic constitution of the human being contains its opposite. On the one hand, images have meaning because there is a subject (a living being) that contemplates them, and on the other, the meaning of the word fades into the semiotic meaning of the linguistic signifier (the acoustic body or the written trace that conveys it). The conscious and the unconscious as psychoanalytic functions of the personality – which is like saying the subjective and inter-subjective poles of the individual or subject as a whole – are thus engaged in a dialectical relationship with each other. You cannot have the one without the other. The key element in the transition, or rather, in this sort of perpetual interplay between figure and ground, and in the *intensification* of one in relation to the other, is the intentional function of *attention*. In the purely human capacity for communication, and in the private but always intersubjective communication that is thought, a language is privileged that is sometimes more "analogical" and sometimes more "digital". According to Vygotskij and Lurija (1984), the main function of language is not to communicate, but to control attention. For them it is important to distinguish between natural attention, which is guided by the stimulus, and language-guided attention, which they call "artificial" attention.

From dream work to dream work alpha and waking dream thought

The German term *Traumarbeit* is often used to refer to the rhetorical mechanisms at work in dream construction as identified by Freud: condensation (*Verdichtung*), displacement (*Verschiebung*), considerations of representability (*Rücksicht auf Darstellbarkeit*) and secondary revision (*sekundäre Bearbeitung*). Dream activity masks the latent thoughts of the dream that may disturb sleep and transforms them into manifest images that have lost their disquieting content. However, it is possible to trace this content by unpacking the way the dream works using the dreamer's associations.

Condensation refers to the fact that a single image can represent an amalgam of several images, as in metaphor; displacement refers to the transfer of investment energy from one image to another (the equivalent of metonymy); figurability, or considerations of representability, refers to the transformation into primarily visual images; finally, secondary revision indicates a sort of final editing process that gives a certain coherence and comprehensibility to the whole, thereby approaching the quality of a daydream.

If the unconscious becomes a psychoanalytic function of the personality, then, Bion concludes, it means that we dream by day as well as by night. Night-time dreaming is only a small part of a much larger and continuous process, which takes place both during waking and sleeping. Waking dream thought is always active. Through alpha function, it continuously translates proto-emotional/sensory experience (or beta elements) into units of meaning (alpha elements). These are not only of a visual nature, as the word pictogram[1] indicates, but also auditory, olfactory, gustatory, tactile and kinesthetic. Initially, the alpha function constructs narrative sequences in the form of images that are real but remain invisible – as if several cards from a pack of Memory cards were placed side by side – except when daydreaming or dream flashes occur in the waking state. On the conscious level, the subject comes up with narrative episodes in words (sensations, feelings, actions), that is to say, narratives that are already "interpretations" of dream sequences: like the glosses of a poetic text that try to apprehend the different levels of meaning all present simultaneously within it.[2] To be able to dream, Bion explains, the dialectic of Kleinian "positions"[3] must be active. He argues that they are negotiated in sleep; in other words the intervention of a "selected fact" (something that surprises the analyst as a possible factor that may bring some clarity to a confusing situation) marks the point of crisis that enables the transition from paranoid and schizoid levels of the mind to depressive levels and vice versa.[4]

With Bion, the theory of dreaming thus changes radically. The dream is no longer, paradoxically, as it was for Freud, an inferior or secondary psychic production whose only function is to inter-cept stimuli that might disturb sleep and which is valuable because it offers an extraordinary window on the unconscious (Meltzer, 1984). Plus, invariably dream work is not done by the primary engine of infantile desire which, through the intervention of cen-sorship, is disguised in the manifest text. For Bion, dreaming is the mode whereby the psyche thinks the real (designated as "O", from "origin", "zero", "vagina", etc.), and thus also thinks and constructs itself. This is why Grotstein (2007; see also Civitarese, 2013a) places it in column 2 of the grid, the column of the falsifi-cation/fabrication/construction of the real (and which naturally can go as far as lying).

Dreaming is ultimately equivalent to "translating" experience, i.e. *thinking*. The dream-alpha builds the "contact barrier", the dynamic and semi-impermeable threshold, made up of alpha elements (our LEGO bricks), which differentiates the unconscious from the conscious and makes for balanced psychic functioning. Basically, it is like a film-maker choosing whether to use macro or wide-angle lenses to shoot a given scene or subject. Only if one is able to transform raw emotions and sensations into alpha elements is it possible to be awake or to fall asleep and to dream. If excessive pressure on either side of the contact barrier (the slash in the Unc/Cs formula), both from the internal world and from factual reality, assumes a traumatic quality, it prevents the proper functioning of the alpha function and of thinking/dreaming. The contact barrier is replaced then by the beta screen, a non-permeable membrane made up of beta elements that surgically separates the unconscious from the conscious. What we then have are different types of psychic suffering, from the all-unconscious of psychosis and hallucination to the hyper-concrete world of people who are cut off from their interiority and the life fluid of their emotions, that is, a more ego-syntonic form of disturbance but in some respects no less malignant than "psychosis". But dreams that do not elicit associations, and realities that are frozen, dried and desiccated are both "similar to hallucinatory proliferations" (Bion, 1992, p. 112).

In Bion's eyes, Freud considered primarily the "negative" aspects of dreams, the processes of concealment and deformation of content, of destruction of meaning, which would otherwise be immediately comprehensible. Bion, on the other hand, emphasizes the positive aspects of elaborating and synthesizing the meaning of experience. There is no conscious perception of reality that is not simultaneously "dreamed", that is, filtered through the creative activity of waking dream thought. Bion is interested in how "the *necessary* dream is *constructed*" (1992, p. 33; Civitarese, 2013b). As Ferro argues, dreams are the psychic elements that have the least need for interpretation-as-deciphering; rather, they are already the more or less successful product of the individual's symbolic/poetic faculties.

There are therefore clear differences between Freud's and Bion's conceptions of the function attributed to dreaming – on the one hand, to hide forbidden thoughts, and on the other, to generate new ideas – that can be variously effective, at the service of the digestion/transformation of emotional experience.

A new theory of affect

Bion accords clear centrality to the emotions (Green, 1998), whereas in Freud it is the empire of the visual and the representational that prevails (Barale, 2008). It is true that with the invention/discovery of transference neurosis, analysis loses the character of a purely cognitive process and becomes an interpersonal and experiential journey. However, Meltzer emphasizes Freud's "absence of a substantial theory of affects throughout his work" (Meltzer, 1984, p. 19), since he sees them "as *manifestations* of meaning and not as *containers* of meaning" (ibid., p. 16).

Melanie Klein is the first to revalue the importance of affects by shifting the focus of the analysis on to the patient's earliest unconscious fantasies active in the here and now and on to the points where anxiety emerges. Unconscious fantasy is always rooted in pre-Oedipal life and is coloured by powerful affects. In spite of this, her approach is still felt to be somewhat abstract and many authors criticize it because ultimately the role of the object (the environment) becomes blurred.

It is only with Bion that unconscious emotional experience in the present takes on real importance. Not only the emotional experience of the patient, but also that of the couple-as-system which they bring into being. At any given moment, emotion signals the weakness or strength of the bond that holds the two members of the dyad together and, in the subject, the different representations within the framework of a coherent Ego. What Bion (1959) describes as an "attack on linking" must be understood above all as an attack on the bond of the relationship. It must be seen in connection with the destruction of the infinite series of interactive micro-"hook-ups" that build the solidity of inferential links generated in thought processes.

As he wished to establish a psychoanalytical science, Freud started from biology and was interested in profound explanations of human behaviour, what he called drives. This is perhaps why Meltzer says that he did not succeed in elaborating a true theory of affect, namely because he sees them most often as products of the discharge of psychic energy. And even if the theory of drives, and the way they press for a differentiation of the psychic, necessarily contains a reference to culture and language – for instance, to the role attributed to word representations that make conscious experience possible – we do not find in Freud the idea that *to make a mind another mind is needed*; at least not in the same terms as in Bion.[5]

If Freud's trajectory has to do with the passage from the pleasure principle to the reality principle, Bion's can be characterized as the shift from the absence of meaning to the intersubjective creation of meaning through lived experience. Bion's theory of thought begins with a concept of truth, understood straight away in a strongly relational sense. The only "drive" that is really present in his work is what Grotstein (2004) calls the "truth drive", where the term drive is now entirely emptied of any connotation of a bridge-concept between the somatic and the psychic, with all the attendant implications of an economic-energetic type. But at its zero degree, this truth, the dawn of any meaning the child may attribute to experience, is represented by unison (*at-one-ment*) with the mother. There is no biological residue in this idea (as there is in the Freudian hydraulics of psychic energies) although the obvious observation can be made that every psychic phenomenon has a corresponding inscription in biological processes. The body in question for Bion is the lived body, the subjective body, the body to which intentionality can be attributed, and which "knows" and "understands" the world in its own way.

Depending on whether they are pleasant/positive or unpleasant/negative, the disturbances represented by waves of undigested or raw emotions push us away from or towards the formless and infinite chaos of matter, of which we necessarily continue to be a part. Emotional experience not only gives meaning to experience but also urges further differentiation. Ogden (2008, p. 12) has summed this up very effectively:

> Bion's theory of thinking is built upon four overlapping and interconnecting principles of mental functioning: (1) thinking is driven by the human need to know the truth – the reality of who one is and what is occurring in one's life; (2) it requires two minds to think a person's most disturbing thoughts; (3) the capacity for thinking is developed in order to come to terms with thoughts derived from one's disturbing emotional experience; and (4) there is an inherent psychoanalytic function of the

personality, and dreaming is the principal process through which that function is performed.

Moreover, unlike Freud, who sees the unconscious as completely alien to the principle of reality, Bion considers, as he himself explains to one of his patients, that "without phantasies and without dreams you have not the means with which to think out your problem" (Bion, 1967, p. 25). At the same time, at-one-ment is related to the maternal capacity for welcoming and "dreaming" the child's anxieties – in essence, for recognizing and loving him.

As can be seen, in Bion's eyes the theory of affects, the theory of the truth drive, the theory of the unconscious and the theory of dreaming are closely interwoven into each other. The essential point to remember is that, for him, emotion always has to do with (human) relationships, and thus with H (hate), L (love), or K (knowledge). As he writes (Bion, 1962a, p. 84): "An emotional experience cannot be conceived of in isolation from a relationship". Here emotion is synonymous with meaning (even when it is aesthetic, semiotic, non-verbal: an initial intersubjective synthesis of multiple proto-emotional and proto-sensory elements) and meaning is a synonym for relationship. The emotional and procedural patterns that begin to order the child's – and later, the adult's – experience of the world, are not only biologically and instinctively determined, but also *always already social and cultural*. There is no meaning possible outside the relationship and every meaning is, on the other hand, necessarily born out of the relationship. By definition, what we call meaning is nothing more than the honey produced by the incessant back-and-forth of the worker bee of conscious and unconscious mutual recognition.

The concept of transformation

Having reviewed in broad strokes Bion's theory of the unconscious, dream, thought and affect, let us now develop the concept of transformation as a *specific* psychoanalytic concept and try to explain why he adopts it. We will then go on to look at the implications for technique in clinical work.

The question is: What is the difference between Freud's principle of dream *distortion* (*Entstellung*) and Bion's principle of *transformation*?

Psychoanalysis doesn't live under a glass fume hood but in the wider context of the society of the time. All great philosophy of the last century, from Husserl and Heidegger to Merleau-Ponty and Derrida, in effect did nothing other than dismantle Cartesian solipsism on the one hand, and the positivist conception of knowledge that springs from it on the other. What in philosophy is tantamount to asserting with force, once and for all, that the *I* is a *we*, and the *we* is I (Hegel, 1807), in psychoanalysis becomes equated with conceiving of the analytic situation no longer as made up of two isolated monads exchanging things, albeit unconsciously, but, as Lacan puts it, as a place where the Ego is the *Other*.

In essence, Freud thinks – obviously, this is in part a simplification – that he is able to capture the reality of the unconscious, of "phantasy", of trauma and of past history because his golden principle is the principle of dream distortion, the only discovery he thinks he has made in complete autonomy (Freud, 1932). Clearly, the term "distortion" contains the idea that something true or *not-distorted* lies behind the dream and is there to be retrieved. Unpacking the work of the dream thus serves to identify the latent, "true" ideas hidden "behind" or "underneath" the deceiving images of dream. The dream, Freud writes, does not think, does not calculate; it merely transforms. Bion has taken this last term seriously, except that he has given it a completely different, and absolutely original, meaning. Unlike for Freud, for him there is no primary truth, historical or unconscious, to be revealed, but only transformations to be carried out that advance the development of the mind(s) and therefore the individual's ability to give a personal meaning to experience.

So, distortion and transformation are very different concepts. Those who say that distortion is also transformation do not get that here it makes sense to speak of transformation only as a specific concept of psychoanalysis and not in its general sense. For Bion and BFT, transformation means that the less we think in terms of causal theories, the better able we are to pay attention to what lies before the eyes of analyst and patient. This is an obvious phenomenological principle: proximity allows us to make observations that we could not otherwise make. The principle is phenomenological because it postulates that in order to enhance a signal, one must shut out what amounts to noise.

Bion develops his concept of transformations as a new theory of observation in psychoanalysis, which he considers as "superior to those already used consciously and unconsciously" (1965, p. 42). The session becomes a dynamic field formed of two minds consciously and unconsciously in contact with each other and continuously pervaded by waves of emotional forces of various kinds and intensity. Like a good surfer, the analyst must pick out the right wave ("the selected fact") and let herself be carried until she makes it safely to shore.

Bion is sharply critical of the traditional approach that looks at history in naively causalistic terms. He sees such an attitude as an example of the "psychosis" of psychoanalysis, which manifests itself in symptoms of arrogance, curiosity and stupidity (Bion, 1958; Civitarese, 2021a). The *hybris* that Bion denounces consists in the pretension to be able to explain in words things that are by definition ineffable. On the theoretical/technical level, this means giving excessive importance to verbal/semantic language and taking insufficient account of the non-verbal, affective, semiotic and aesthetic side of language.

Let us then ask ourselves the question: What is distinctive about the concept of transformation? A glance at the subtitle of *Transformations* – which is both a theoretical manifesto and a research programme – and we immediately understand more: *Change from Learning to Growth*. At one fell swoop, Bion outlines a theoretical change that underlies his idea that in some way classical psychoanalysis has exhausted its possibilities, and that for this reason we must start again from the beginning. Today we would sum it up as a shift from the "evidential paradigm" (Ginzburg, 1986) to the aesthetic paradigm (Civitarese, 2014), from the psychoanalysis of suspicion to the psychoanalysis of respect (Nissim Momigliano, 1992); or again, from a model of the development of the psyche based on drive satisfaction to a model based on intersubjective[6] recognition – a process of becoming subjects that unfolds through partial reciprocal self-alienation. This is what Bion does: it is not our animality in itself that is questioned, but the way it is introduced into the human order of sense and meaning. Trying to "get to know" the cause of psychic suffering means understanding what is not working at *that* level. It is a transition from the intrapsychic to the intersubjective or transindividual, from distortion to transformation.

One could, of course, also find equivalent formulas: "from *knowing about* reality to *becoming real*" (Bion, 1965, p. 153); in the manner of Kant, to be interested more in the *how* than in the *what* of thinking; more in *being* than in *knowing*; shifting from a psychoanalysis that deals with the deformations of representations of reality thought to be true to a psychoanalysis that deals with the processes of transformation through which a conviction about what is true matures intersubjectively; from a psychoanalysis that aims to make conscious the unconscious to a psychoanalysis that aims to make unconscious the conscious, and so on. In order to express this concept – to begin a process of learning from experience that will enrich the subject's un/conscious capacity for symbolization – Bion invents the active verb "to unconscious", although he only uses it in the past participle, "unconscioused", to translate the German word *unbewusst*, "unconscious" (Bion, 1992, p. 353), or he writes that one has to be *at one* with reality.

If this is the more general framework of discourse, we find a more detailed response in *Transformations*: "The analyst's main concern must be with the material of which he has direct evidence, namely, the emotional experience of the analytical sessions themselves. It is in his approach to this experience that the concepts of transformation and invariance can play an illuminating role" (Bion, 1965, p. 7).

Let us try to summarize some of Bion's main theoretical principles:

a   only that which is under the eyes of analyst and patient is available for investigation and transformation;

b   by definition, this something, the "O" common to analyst and patient, is the couple's actual unconscious emotional experience or, as it were, their "basic assumption";

c   however, the emotional experience shared by the couple can never be known because it is "ultimate reality", a thing in itself; it only represents the origin (the "O") of possible transformations; if we could "see" something and how that something "really" is, we would not need the concept of transformation;

d   the concept of transformation is the most useful when approaching the emotional experience of the session. At the manifest level, transformations can be of the patient or of the analyst; those of the analyst (interpretations) are transformations from a psychoanalytic point of view.

However, there is at least one other point in *Transformations* where Bion makes clear why he places this concept at the centre of his thinking:

> I make no claim for objective reality, as far as I understand the meaning usually attributed to the term, but for me, a factual situation (conjectured) an emotional state (say hate, also conjectured) a representation (Tp β) are constantly conjoined and I record (grid E3) or bind (grid E1) it by the term "transformation".
>
> It follows from the theory of transformations that whenever I see one element of the equation O, Tp α, Tp β + L, or H or K, the others must be present. But I shall *not* assume that one causes the other, though for convenience I may (as I have already done when I used the phrase "because of the hatred", etc., p. 68) employ a theory of causation to express myself. Indeed the object of binding what seems to be a constant conjunction of elements by a name "transformation" is in the hope of discovering the meaning of the constant conjunction.
>
> (1965, pp. 68–69)

So, saying *meaning* is different from saying *cause*. The first term refers to a pragmatic theory of truth, while the second refers to a representationalist theory (to the idea of "objective reality"). In this passage Bion states a new method: I see as if for the first time which elements are usually found together in a configuration, and then I check whether this is recurrent. Therefore, when I later see only some of them, I can propose the hypothesis of the presence of the others even when they are not visible.

What does such an approach, which we can call "phenomenological", entail? Like Husserl, Bion seems to think that of the three unrelated modes whereby we experience the object – *signitive* (through linguistic acts), *representational* (through likenesses) and *perceptual* – only the third is that which gives us the thing in flesh and blood (*leibhaftig*). When we are in the presence of another person, we manage to have an empathic understanding of his state of mind which has a quasi-perceptual character, as reflected in such common expressions as "green with rage" or "red with shame". This understanding, which, if biunivocal, can also be termed *unison*, comes about through "coupling" (a "mutual transfer of sense" or "mutual awakening" (p. 133), analogical transposition or "cross-modal matching" (Zahavi, 2014, p. 157). When using such an approach, a principle of unity of experience is at stake. In a certain sense, all models of psychoanalysis, and especially its relational models, are based on a similar phenomenological reduction, but in a more partial way and, above all, mostly retaining a traditional notion of subject and unconscious. Not the unconscious as Bion outlines it, seen as a psychoanalytic function of the personality, but the repressed unconscious of classical theory.

In all this, of course, Bion starts again from Melanie Klein and the brilliant innovation of comparing children's play to adult dreaming. Playing in infant analysis involves a series of concepts that are really only made explicit in Bion. In play everything is a game (everything in the session is part of the fictional world of the dream); in the "psychoanalytic game" the analyst is fully involved and the narratives that unfold are the outcome of the contribution made by all the players; the game provides rules that have been previously agreed — and even if the rules were invented at that moment, those that belong to the larger relational game that serves as a backdrop to the game itself would not cease to exist. What matters in the game is not the main characters or the plots but rather how one learns to symbolize (to dream, to think – to translate experience) by contriving stories; in the theatre of the internal world live internal objects (characters) that are constantly at work weaving patterns that then give meaning to the experience of the external world. These internal objects do not coincide totally with representations, but express the procedural patterns that have gradually been inscribed in the body since the primary relationship; the idea of the extent and precociousness of transference as a total situation; the proto-intersubjective concept of projective identification, etc.

By adopting this point of view, Bion tries to remedy what typically happens, for example, when an analyst reads a patient's history, but also the protocols of the sessions, when certain facts are immediately linked to supposed events in a close causal relationship. It then happens that the field of the unknown – not anything vague and generic, but the shared unconscious emotional experience – becomes immediately filled with what is already known. The concept of transformation, which emphasizes the significance of phenomenological observation – and avoids slipping into the opposite conceptions that base the universalism of knowledge entirely on the object (ingenuous realism) or on the subject (naive idealism) – departs from establishing an immediate and "obvious" relationship of cause and effect. In this way, it defensively avoids collapsing the process of signification into some expected traumatic theory.

As we shall see more clearly below, this is one of the main reasons why Bion introduces the concept of O in *Transformations*, namely to assert with great force a principle of systematic doubt, the functional value of which is to bring analytic listening to new heights of receptivity, and to overcome the "myth" of historical or objective data.

Accordingly, in itself the term "transformation" conveys several ideas:

a   the idea of process, of something that takes place between A and B, not only in A, nor only in B;
b   paying "epistemological" attention to the modes of knowledge, which echoes the transition from pre-critical to critical philosophy, which in Bion becomes a theory of thought – that is, a theory that, above all else, questions the very faculty of knowing;
c   the crisis of any metaphysical or positivist claims (the idea of being able to identify an ultimate truth) because the O which is subject to transformation is never directly attainable;
d   against all superficial eclecticism, the claim to the legitimacy of formulating more appropriate theories to describe the facts of the analysis, provided that the vertex adopted is scientific and not dogmatic; and consequently, within a Kuhnian perspective, also of (respectful) competition between theories;
e   last but not least, the need to coin new terms to describe the same things (obviously they can never be "the same"), to compensate for the wear and tear suffered by the already

existing terms. This is where Bion's major recourse to the intertextual knowledge of logic, philosophy, mathematics, mysticism and literature has its origin; first and foremost the aim is to serve his own objectives, that is, to be of use to the psychoanalytic vertex. Not unlike Freud, Bion is the living example, which all analysts should follow, of a fruitful intellectual nomadism.

Let us now take up some of the above points in more detail and ask the following questions: if Bion forswears the idea of "objective reality", how does he manage to maintain any idea of truth? How can he make it, as he puts it, the "food of the mind". And lastly, how can he posit truth as the only "drive" he wishes to develop?

What do we mean when we say that the only thing that counts is the O of the session?

If the point of arrival of theoretical developments in psychoanalysis is, as we have tried to describe, the maximum possible regard for the analyst's subjectivity ("the common thread", as we called it, in the history of psychoanalysis) vis-à-vis that of the patient, this means that the only thing that counts in analysis is to pay attention to what happens in the here and now, and to the shared unconscious emotional climate (O). *Why is this the case?* Because every time we digress from the here and now, we slip back into objectifying the patient once again — it is in effect as if we stopped looking in the most radical and inclusive way possible at the role of our unconscious in determining the fact to be investigated. Bion, however, speaks about the O of the session in ways that many find confusing. We need to simplify things a bit. Do we want to understand what O is? Then we must become familiar with Bion's group theory. Bion tells us that groups behave as a unit, as one entity, when they are pervaded by strong unconscious emotions, which he calls "basic assumptions". Some of these basic assumptions (in the *sophisticated* or *work group*) lead to development, others to regression (*fight/flight* or *dependent*). Of course, none of these assumptions is ever pure.

Let us think of a hospital psychiatric team that occasionally stops being therapeutic because it is periodically affected by explosive emotions. Dangerous actings-out, violence, failure to pass on information, etc., come into play. The main work of a psychiatric team (but by the same token of any group) is to carry out the maintenance that enables it to become a working group again. There are no shortcuts to achieving this goal. The only way is to provide a self-observation/supervision function. If we think about how groups work, it is easy for us to think that they can behave as a unit, for example in attack or escape mode, etc. Why then do we find it so difficult to think of the analytic couple – or, as we say, the dyad – as a real group?

In fact, the subject is itself already an internal group of individuals, resulting from infinite previous identifications, which are in constant dialogue with each other; and even two concrete individuals function according to the same laws of the group. Again, do we want to understand what constitutes the O of the session? A pragmatic and useful approximation to Bion's concept might be to think of it as the basic assumption of the analyst–patient "group" in the session. If we admit that this basic assumption – about the emotional weather or atmosphere – can be extremely positive or extremely constructive, we understand that it is important to have an idea of what potential mathematical sign every moment has before it, whether plus (+) or minus (–). It goes without saying that, as in the example of a psychiatric working group, or a football team, etc., if the sign is minus (–) we have to bring it back to plus (+); or, using Kleinian terminology, from PS (paranoid-schizoid position) to D (depressive position). The plus sign (+) indicates that the group-mind grows (and likewise that of the individuals that comprise it) because it is able to accept new ideas without disintegrating and without losing its identity, but rather by encouraging the process of subjectivation.

What is the meaning of transformations in O and K?

The difference is explained by what was outlined above. Merely intellectual knowledge (K) that is not based on the experience lived in the session (O) is mutilated. There are two reasons for this: (a) because it applies mostly to something that is already known and not to what is unknown, thus only satisfying a desire to possess a kind of detached knowledge *about* the other instead of engaging in a living relationship; b) because it is more easily separated from affective, bodily knowledge, which is only triggered when the analyst rediscovers that, like the patient, she is one of the main actors on stage. Most people who ask for an analysis suffer precisely from a kind of de-personalization or split between abstract (intellectual) and emotional (bodily) thinking. The intellectual defences against anxiety become hypertrophic because they are used to compensate for deficiencies in emotional or bodily knowledge, which is normally referred to in terms of the concept of affective or relational competence.

For the analyst, the problem is how to gain access to this plane of being which is not that of the abstract meaning of language but which is represented by patterns or forms of so-called implicit or procedural knowledge. It is clear that psychoanalytic interpretation always has an intellectual component. It is then a question of seeing whether this intellectual content is a presumed hidden truth (if it is limited to K) or whether it is something that leads precisely to O, that is, to learning from emotional experience; if it encourages an alternative game of interaction and immersion, or if it fosters the former to the detriment of the latter. Bion and BFT postulate that the emotional atmosphere in the consulting room is always impregnated with *love* (L) or *hatred* (H); in other words, it is progressive or regressive (Civitarese, 2020, 2021a). This is the basic dialectical pair that governs the analytic process, since in itself the third entity, *knowledge* (K) can be a promoter of both love and hatred.

Intersubjectivity and BFT

The concept of intersubjectivity is a good way to recapitulate the current paradigm of psychoanalysis. Analysts have followed Husserl (and sometimes Hegel – who however, used the different term of recognition/*Anerkennung*) – in differentiating themselves from models of psychoanalysis based on the Cartesian conception of the isolated subject who solipsistically tries to understand himself. The whole philosophy of the last century attempts to throw Descartes off his pedestal, and in my opinion succeeds in doing so very well.

It makes no sense to think of the individual unless within a group. What we call subject or *Dasein* or *Being-there* is like a coin with two faces that cannot be separated from each other and that conventionally we may call "subjectivity" and "intersubjectivity" (Civitarese, 2021b). The relationship between the two faces is dialectical, that is to say, one cannot exist without the other. We cannot say that subjectivity as the subject's individual polarity comes first and then later comes intersubjectivity, or vice versa. From the beginning, since mere matter has been subjected to the transformative action of opposing forces of nature, they are either both there or not there. This is true both for pre-reflexive or prelinguistic subjectivity and intersubjectivity (as in the case of animals), and for linguistic subjectivity and intersubjectivity (fully human).

The key point is that intersubjectivity should not be understood as the mere interaction of two distinct individuals. It would be banal to make such an assertion – there would be no *there* there. Rather, it should be interpreted as referring to the existence of a *common* background that is both biological/instinctual and linguistic/cultural, that is to say, homogeneous and indistinct in nature. What Husserl investigated his entire life under the heading intersubjectivity, Freud investigated under the heading "unconscious". We see ourselves as monads, autonomous subjects and the hub of our own thoughts and activities – that is *the visible*. The difficult point is to see *the invisible* of intersubjectivity or the unconscious. Husserl and Freud, both students of the philosopher Brentano (Aenishanslin, 2019), started from the isolated subject, as if they were seeking to radicalize the position of Descartes' Cogito, but they were both forced to consider that being a "subject" means *being subject* to something; to what if not to the Other?

Different models of psychoanalysis declare themselves intersubjective but then fall to a greater or lesser extent under the paradigm of a one-person and not a group psychology (as opposed to "relational" or "bi-personal"). Another misunderstanding is to think that intersubjectivity means total symmetry between patient and analyst. If it makes sense to postulate symmetry on the unconscious plane of the relationship, it certainly does not make sense on the conscious plane; yet this same distinction should be dialecticized, if it is true that conscious and unconscious can be represented as the two sides of a Möbius strip – in actual fact one side rotating through 180 degrees. In conclusion, knowing what is meant by intersubjectivity in philosophy, from Hegel to Husserl and Merleau-Ponty, helps us refine our concepts of "third", "field", unconscious as infinite (Bion, 1965), or *common* or *shared* unconscious, and draw a coherent technique for clinical work from it.

Why is BFT more radically intersubjective than others?

BFT does not limit the plane on which an event can be seen as intersubjective, symmetrical, co-generated or co-constructed *to a circumscribed sphere* of the relationship – outside of which, in the session, a (naively) realistic view of things continues to exist. Instead, *as a postulate*, it rigorously considers that virtually *anything* can be interpreted from the perspective of an unconscious event in the field, and not only that which is attributable to a split-off aspect of the patient's personality. When this aspect is called into play, ultimately the constitution of the field is traced back to the patient's pathology. But wouldn't this contradict the basic principle of the symmetry of the unconscious field?

Let me give an example. If a patient tells me a dream, I don't consider it only as the dream that the patient had at night at home, which may already be relevant in itself, but I consider the dream story as part of the dream that I myself, together with the patient, am having in the here and now by transforming beta elements of nonsense into verbal elements and meaningful representations. *No matter who tells the dream* (or who the reverie or hallucinosis belongs to), it is still a dream we are dreaming together.

Another example: a patient tells me about a traumatic episode from his childhood, and this already tells me a lot about him and his personality. But, by adding on another lens, I parenthesize this information, as it were (or put in the background), and treat it *as if* it were a dream narrative that we are having together in real time. Why do I do this? Because then it is easier for me to intuit the emotional experience that the story expresses and go on to bring it back into the analytic field. A whole series of relevant consequences, both theoretical and technical, follow from this move.

Container/contained

Thought up by Bion, this formula, deployed to describe the nature and quality of the link between two terms, is brilliant both in its simplicity and its correspondence to the experience of practical life. Examples of concrete relationships (Bion also uses the symbols for female and male: ♀♂) are: mouth/nipple, vagina/penis, group/individual, mother/child etc. Container/contained relations are always multiple and reciprocal, as well as being virtually infinite if we also consider the small scale of interaction. The child contains in its mouth the nipple, which contains milk, while at the same time it is held by the arms of the mother, while both exist in broader contexts that sustain and support them, and so on. ♀♂ is an extremely powerful and versatile tool. If it is heir to the concept of projective identification, then Bion reshapes it as a sexual metaphor, as can also be seen from the symbols he chooses to represent it, or as a metaphor of the mind as a digestive apparatus. It immediately gives an idea of what can happen if too much content (contained) is forced into an inadequate container – or also, vice versa, if the container has become infinite and is no longer really able to accommodate and give form (meaning) to the contained.

If we are to answer this key question, we need to have in mind the model of the mother–*infant* relationship (I purposely do not say "mother–child"). The mother is able to give a mind to the child starting from when she does not yet understand the meaning of the words. It can only be an attunement based on the music of proprioceptive and exteroceptive sensations, the first rudiments of emotions, nascent patterns of action and habits, etc. At the centre are processes of mutual affective regulation, the negotiation of primordial or non-verbal "concepts". We said that Bion puts emotion back at the heart of psychoanalysis, whereas in Freud the same role is played by representation. The focus is on the processes of progression/regression that characterize a group (even just of two people) and that are determined by the interplay of basic assumptions. Bion's psychoanalysis is anti-intellectualistic. The objective is to identify the basic assumption in order to modify it. A mind is born and grows every time order is created, and this can only happen socially. Making a mind expand means widening the unconscious, which Bion understands as the psychoanalytic function of the personality responsible for giving meaning to lived experience. No longer translating from unconscious to conscious but rather the opposite. The unconscious is no longer seen as a sort of Dante's inferno encapsulated in the individual, but as the dimension of pre-linguistic and linguistic intersubjectivity that interacts dialectically with the dimension of pre-linguistic and linguistic subjectivity, and thus enables the process of becoming subjects to unfold. The distance from Freud may seem unbridgeable, but – I repeat – it is not so if we transition through the equation set up by Melanie Klein between dream and play, and between play and symbolization work.

Ideally, a *psychic growth index* (PGI) could be measured at the end of each session, in the same way as the Dow Jones Index (DJI) is calculated when Wall Street closes down for the day. And it would reflect the increment in the subject's feeling of agency or power to feel and act as a free human being, something which mostly occurs cumulatively (*cumulative growth*) and thus also unnoticed.

Notes

1 The second element that enters into the creation of the word, "gram", comes from the Greek γραμμα, which is derived from γράφω "to write".
2 The narrative derivatives of waking dream thought are like the waves of an echocardiogram. They show transmodal correspondences with the anatomy of the heart, but not perfect isomorphy.
3 The paranoid-schizoid position (PS) is a mental state in which anxiety and confusion dominate, but also openness to the new; in the depressive position (D), what dominates is integration and awareness, but also a certain stagnation. In non-pathological conditions there is always an ongoing and discrete oscillation from one position to another and back again.
4 A "selected fact" is like an opportunity for a profitable stock market investment that is thought to be about to increase in value; in our case, meaning and agency.
5 See A. Green (1998, p. 656):
    Bion's conception of the object is quite personal. It is not Freud's and it is also different from Klein's. Though it may sound abstract, it is in fact more plausible than many others. For Bion the direct feeding relationship, which relates to the breast, can't explain the richness of the experience. The mother feeds the infant not only with her milk or her breast, she nourishes him also psychically, she daydreams feelings and "mental" states about the child. And so she enables the child to reintroject his own projections that are now changed through her.
6 Throughout the book I use this term in both its adjectival and nominative form, in two different ways, which the reader will be able to

distinguish according to the context: at the descriptive or phenomen-ological level, where it refers to the simple interaction between two people; or, at the ontological or metapsychological level, where it refers to the layer of identity that unites them, also called "transcendental" since it goes beyond the reach of both consciousness and the separate existence of each individual. In this second meaning, the inter-subjectivity of the subject correlates dialectically with the subjectivity of the subject, which instead expresses its separateness. These distinc-tions are important because they help us overcome the false dichotomy between the individuality of the individual and the "groupishness" of the individual. As we see, the term "subject" has a similarly ambiguous status, which can be clarified as needs be by distinguishing between its common use (subject as an empirical being) and its speculative use, which has to do with its structure.

Chapter 3

The model of mother–infant relationship

In BFT the model of care is the process whereby a new mind is created in the mother–child relationship. It is therefore worth devoting some space to this model before going on to review some of the working tools. Unlike Freud, and with Winnicott, but, compared to the latter, perhaps in a less "clinical" and more theoretical way, Bion places the mother–child relationship at the centre of psychoanalysis as the model of how a mind is created for the first time and how it then develops. This is one of the major innovations contained in his essay "The Psycho-Analytic Study of Thinking" (1962b); and it goes along with the rejection of the binary opposition between primary and secondary processes, and the introduction of the concept of alpha function. Rather than a mother–child model, however, we should speak of a mother–infant model. In fact, the term "infant" denotes a child that is not yet able to understand the abstract meaning of words. If we focus on this stage of the relationship, we obtain a clearer explanatory model also of non-verbal communication in adult psychoanalysis, an aspect whose centrality we have realized over time in any analysis and with any kind of patient.

The idea we all have of how mother and infant communicate is based on the concept of container/contained. This is one of Bion's most well-known, simple, versatile and effective metaphors. The child transmits its anxieties to the mother. If the mother is sufficiently permeable and capable of reverie, she allows these anxieties to stay inside her for a time and transforms them. Once they have

DOI: 10.4324/9781003219972-3

been "mitigated", or digested, she returns them in a form that the child can handle. If, on the other hand, the mother is not capable of reverie (not in the conventional sense of fantasizing but rather as a way of loving, of looking at the other with a gaze suffused with affection and imbued with "preconceptions" of what the child will become), the same anxieties ricochet back in heightened form and become "nameless terror". The expression is apt because it suggests the particular inhibition that can affect the development of symbolic thought in the child – not having words for things, or being name-*less.*

Sometimes this model is understood in a sense that is too unidirectional and does not sufficiently contemplate the reciprocity that marks the relationship both when things are going quite well and when they are not. Firstly, let us start with a clarification. When we say that the mother "contains" the anxieties of the child, this is not to be thought of as a merely intentional process, in the sense of consciousness. Everything travels along communication channels that cannot be controlled directly. This immediately clears the field of simplistic ways of interpreting notions such as *at-one-ment*, "containment" or even "recognition". Secondly, let us ask ourselves the question: are we more convinced by the idea of acceptance-and-restitution or rather by the idea of a "dance" in which mother and child at a certain point synchronize their movements and expressions, so that in the end what we have is a dynamic *system* capable to a greater or lesser degree of transforming the emotional turbulence that pervades it? The dance would not unfold if only the child or only the mother were present.

For example, Merleau-Ponty, whose entire oeuvre, in the wake of Husserl, amounts to an attempt to transcend the subject/object dichotomy that besets psychology, would not agree at all with Bion that emotions are not *sense-able* (Civitarese, 2015a). On the contrary, he believes that emotions can always be read in the other, that they are always expressed in the body and in actions. As he writes:

> we must reject the prejudice which makes "inner realities" out of love, hate, or anger, leaving them accessible to one single witness: the person who feels them. Anger, shame, hate, and

love are not psychic facts hidden at the bottom of another's consciousness: they are types of behavior or styles of conduct which are visible from the outside. They exist *on* that face or *in* those gestures, not hidden behind them ... emotion is not a psychic, internal fact, but rather a variation in our relations with others and the world which is expressed in our bodily attitude.

(Merleau-Ponty, 1945b, pp. 52–53)

Elsewhere, he adds that "vision is a palpation with the look ... the thickness of flesh between the seer and the thing is constitutive for the thing of its visibility as for the seer of his corporeity; it is not an obstacle between them, it is their means of communication" (Merleau-Ponty, 1964, pp. 134–135); or that "the seer and the visible reciprocate one another and we no longer know which sees and which is seen" (ibid., p. 139).

What is generated then, as in the case of the elements that make up the figures studied by Gestalt psychology, is an "autonomous" intercorporeity: like a musical motif (whether found or invented). Winnicott might say that each separately can anticipate the end, and thus that they are immediately influenced by it and feel enveloped and contained by it. Fuchs and De Jaegher describe this process as follows:

When two individuals interact ... the coordination of their body movements, utterances, gestures, gazes, etc. can gain such momentum that it overrides the individual intentions, and common sense-making emerges ... The "in-between" becomes the source of the operative intentionality of both partners. Each of them behaves and experiences differently from how they would do outside of the process, and meaning is co-created in a way not necessarily attributable to either of them.

(2009, p. 476)

So, the dance unfolds according to a principle of reversibility or re-flexion. Similarly, if I touch my left hand with my right, what I get is not only a feeling but a sensation, since the touched hand is itself endowed with sensitivity and touches the touching hand; and if I touch, feel and see another what I get is a different but analogous kind of reversibility or reflexivity. What in the first case constitutes all my own flesh, in the second case constitutes the "flesh of the world" (Merleau-Ponty, 1964). Visibility, the very possibility that perception (sensitivity) is given, resides in this chiasmatic structure of experience.

It seems to me that this vision is more convincing than that of a mere interaction between mother and child, however dense the exchanges may be. But then we would no longer say that the mother contains the child's emotionality in a one-way direction, and it is occasionally the child who must take on the mother's anxieties. Rather, we would think of a *field* constituted by the movements of the mother–child pair; a structure or device that as a whole sometimes promotes the growth of both and sometimes hinders it; that is to say, it can function in either a progressive or regressive sense.

There is an obvious objection to the point I am making: the symbolic capacities of mother and infant differ vastly. This is true. Still, if we try to imagine situations of real interaction, are we sure that, for example, the ability on the part of the child, obviously *at his or her level (or "style" of being)*, to respond to the stimulations of the mother is not just as powerful in containing her anxieties as, when necessary, are her reflective capacities in containing the child? Or, on the other hand, are we sure that a lack of responsiveness *on the part of the child* is not as disorganizing for the mother as a lack of emotional responsiveness on the part of the mother is for the child? What I am trying to say is that when we try to build more persuasive models of the vicissitudes of the mother–child relationship, perhaps we should take a much more holistic, intersubjective and egalitarian view than we usually do. Thinking in these terms, I believe, helps us symmetrize the mother–infant and analyst–patient relationship, and also gain a more meaningful appreciation of the value of non-verbal communication.

If we assume that the child depends on the mother much more than the mother depends on the child, perhaps we will be able to better grasp the significance of the special dance they perform together if we set aside this kind of difference. If we think about the way Hegel conceptualizes the dynamics of recognition using the model of the servant–master dialectic, what is surprising is that the master has everything and the servant has only his state of dependence. Thus, in the ingenious examples that Hegel draws from literature to illustrate his thesis, Creon is the lord of the city and Antigone, on the other hand, has no concrete power; likewise, Rameau's nephew is totally dependent on the wealthy Bertin. However, to understand what it means to "recognize" each other is to understand that *on a fundamental level* all these differences disappear. The mutual recognition that structures an affective bond does not admit of hierarchies. In the words Freud relegates to a footnote in *Civilization and its Discontents* (1930, p. 130), it is based on the experience of being loved (*Liebeserfahrung*). This would not be the case if only the concrete element and only symbolic skills counted.

As we know, Winnicott (1965) mentions the child's state of double dependence (material and spiritual) on the mother. But we should also talk more about *the mother's* dependence on the child. Perhaps not "double", if we want to exclude the material aspect, but certainly emotional. If we then think of the forms of psychic suffering that the mother can also experience when things do not go well, then here too we could speak of a double dependence, in the sense that the possible failure of the relationship may end up having consequences that are not only spiritual.

What do we gain if we adopt a less unidirectional approach, in other words, if we not only postulate, with Winnicott, that a child does not exist (unless seen together with the mother), but also try to go beyond a "relational" or merely interactive vision? In my opinion, such a view is implicit in the following point made by Bion: "The mother's capacity for reverie is the receptor organ for the infant's harvest of self-sensation gained by its [rudimentary] consciousness" (1962b, p. 309). If the mother's evolved consciousness and the child's rudimentary consciousness overlap, it means that we are postulating *a whole* that is more than the sum of its constituent parts. So, to set aside the concrete differences between mother and infant and the large divide between their abstract symbolic capacities is a move that would not make sense if we were evaluating, for example in a court of law, the responsibilities of each member of the couple in terms of the quality of the relationship. Given that our aim is to focus as sharply as possible on the dynamics of the mother–child interaction on the emotional level, this sort of phenomenological option helps us see things we would not otherwise see.

It allows us, for example, to tune in better to the mother's suffering and to indulge less in guilt-ridden attitudes, which as we know are so common as to be the source of witticisms ("analysts are always mad at mothers"). The "overestimation" of the mother's role stems from the overestimation of abstract thought and the epistemic side of analysis as opposed to the ontological, affective or "becoming" side. What I am trying to propose is in line with Bion, namely *to privilege a descriptive or observational view over a genetic or causal view*. The idea is that the latter can fatally conceal the former.

If we then transpose what we have said into adult psychoanalysis, we should likewise set aside all too clear characterizations of the analyst as containing the patient or of the patient as only occasionally containing the analyst (Bion's concept of "best colleague"). In this way we would have a more convincing model of how the dance, as I have called it, plays out on the unconscious plane of the relationship. It is obvious that mother and analyst consciously try to direct the relationship towards an idea of "care" – in the two senses of "caring for" and care as therapy. However, it would be limiting not to change perspective when we enter the field of processuality and the *unconscious* phenomena of the session.

To this end, in my opinion, it may be useful to embrace the idea of intercorporeity, as proposed by Merleau-Ponty. Perhaps we should think of projective identification as opening up connections, channels of communication, arterial and venous vessels that constitute an interface, as with the placenta in foetal life, always and "automatically" travelled in both directions. We would then more easily have the image of a *whole*, of a *functional pairing*, and not of contents that "jump" from one subject to another across an immaterial medium. It is no coincidence that, as we saw, behind the model of the container/contained there is the sexual metaphor of coitus, and therefore, ultimately, of ecstasy/sensual union. If projective identification is used to conceptualize this functional entity, we get a vivid image of how the container expands and how in fact we are part of a community whose members are connected by threads and whose essence we can only appreciate if we imagine it as *carnal* and not merely "spiritual" (as early as 1945b Merleau-Ponty was writing: "I am a field, I am an experience", p.

429, and elsewhere: "I am an intersubjective field", p. 478; or: "just as the parts of my body together form a system, the other's body and my own are a single whole, two sides of a single phenomenon, and the anonymous existence, of which my body is continuously the trace, henceforth inhabits these two bodies simultaneously", p. 370). Without flesh or corporeality or sensibility there would be no Spirit. If we were to prefer *this* "scientific fiction" to Freud's notion (1911) of the child seen in isolation as a bird in its egg, this would give us an even fresher understanding of Winnicott's famous phrase about there being no child without a mother.

At the last Venice Biennale (2019), the Azerbaijan artists Kanan Aliyev and Ulviyya Aliyeva[1] presented *The Slinky Effect* ("slinky" also means furtive, stealthy, secret, libidinous, etc.), an installation with figures of women and men connected by a large spring that went from one figure's head to another. The intention was to make people think about the alienating aspects of virtual reality. For our purposes, this image adequately depicts an anti-Cartesian idea of subjectivity. After all, projective identification is the means for channelling both the alienation that constitutes the subject and that which undermines it.

Actually, Kanan Aliyev's image is still too relational; it still seems to be too much about the connection between separate "heads". Perhaps the idea I want to suggest can be better conveyed by two paintings by Guariento, one entitled *Group of Ten Angels* and the other *Array of Armed Angels*, to be found in the Musei Eremitani in Padua. They show superimposed nimbuses.

Sometimes depicted as girded with rays, the golden discs symbolize the light of the Spirit that permeates all the angels and unites them into a single entity. My aim here is to construct a model of the mother–infant relationship, but equally of *any other* relationship, one which is built on how Bion depicts the process of projective identification↔mother's capacity for reverie/alpha function, but also on the pervasive group inspiration of his thinking, and especially on the emphasis on emotion as a sensitive concept or idea, primordial abstraction, the idea of truth as food for the mind.

Going down this path, one might also believe that compared to Winnicott's approach, which shows us the real child interacting with the mother (one need only think of the amazing concept of the transitional object, the piece of cloth with a soothing quality that we all loved and cherished), Bion's "theoretical" child is paradoxically closer to this essential dimension of intercorporeity and *embodied* intersubjectivity, which will later lead to the developments of BFT.

It is important to mention, however, that the technique Bion inaugurated and that was then developed by later authors really puts Winnicott's famous principle into practice in a way that Winnicott himself perhaps does not. For Winnicott, mother and child form a system but this system does not come to be conceptualized as a field in the radical sense that, as we have seen, Merleau-Ponty attributes to this term. The reference to Merleau-Ponty is in no way random since he is at the origin of the Barangers' field theory and very close to Bion's conception of dreams and the unconscious. A possible explanation for this paradox is that, as usual, Bion arrives at the mother–child pair/group starting from the study of small groups. Bion sees projective identification as a form of communication that is normal, *simultaneous* and in fact always two-way, but we could equally well extend this interpretation to include what is outside the realm of "normal".

This is why, in my view, the concept of introjective identification is not used very much: because it has already been incorporated into that of projective identification. If I remove something from myself in order to place it in the other, I am not only partially alienating him from himself but I am in turn being modified/negated by the other. Put differently, the concept of projective identification is inherently dialectical. And of course, one should never forget that Bion's intersubjectivism is based on a radical revision of the concept of the unconscious and the dream. In essence, my thesis is that in Bion the model of group functioning is always active as a secret theoretical operator, perhaps unconsciously, both in the model of the mother–infant relationship and, more generally, in all subsequent developments of his thinking (Civitarese, 2021c).

To sum up, the point I have made here is that Bion's view of the mother–infant relationship has, on the one hand, had a major impact in changing the paradigm of contemporary psychoanalysis, while on the other, if we only think about the developments of BFT, we see that it has also played an extra-ordinary heuristic function. Let me quickly run through the essential points of my argument:

a   Projective identification as the model of even normal non-verbal communication (as Bion pointed out) can be read as a complete *psychoanalytic* theory of what Hegel calls the dialectic of recognition, a term we can consider as synonymous with at-one-ment.

b   In "The Psycho-Analytic Study of Thinking" (1962b) Bion proffers an extraordinary dialectical model which intuits the origin of temporality starting from the game of *thing/no-thing* or *breast/no-breast* vs. *noughtness,* and from the principle of tolerance of the frustration caused by the absence of the object (Civitarese, 2019a). In this regard, I repeat, it is essential to start from the model of the mother–infant, and not from the mother–child relationship. That is to say, we must ask how a child who does not understand the meaning of words can develop a mind.

c   Bion emphasizes the meaning of emotion as a "concept" or "sensitive idea" (body schema, implicit memory, etc.), emotional truth *negotiated* by the couple and food that nourishes the mind. When positive, the emotion expresses the bonding pleasure that comes from mutual recognition.

d   With the group inspiration of his thinking, Bion inaugurates a true psychoanalysis of intercorporeity or intersubjectivity – not to be understood as a simple interaction but as a dynamic field. This is the sense in which I re-interpret the container/contained relationship. Bion gives us the tools to go beyond the Cartesian view of the subject as a disembodied transcendental ego, and thus to develop a more convincing theory of the subject as a lived body, the unconscious as the symbolic function of the personality and dreams as the poetry of mind-and-body. None of this comes into being ready-made in Bion, like Minerva from the head of Jupiter; what we need to do is to understand the seeds that later came together and blossomed into the developments of his thinking we find in BFT.

e   Bion forcefully puts forward the mother–infant relationship, and therefore the way in which a mind can be developed even when the child has not yet acquired language, *as a model also for adult psychoanalysis.* It follows that perhaps we should revise our one-way model of the mother who "contains" and transforms the child's anxieties. From a certain point of view, the child is able from birth to enter into a rich dialogue that immediately becomes *something more* than a mere interaction between separate subjects (although the child is not a subject in the proper sense; here it is a matter of how *we* conceive the relationship). Right away the child, in the same way as it is contained by her, "contains" the mother's anxieties, reinforces her on the level of identity, satisfies her deepest desires, etc. Ultimately, then, what contains the anxieties of both is the rhythm and harmony (the music) of the relational dance they perform together, seen as the possibility of social understanding that "emerges from a dynamical process of interaction and coordination of two embodied subjects coupled to each other" (Fuchs and De Jaegher, 2009, p. 470). The "common space" that is thus created continuously oscillates from moments of *synchronization* (attunement; unison; or, as a patient of mine once put it, "quality moments"), when one is "in phase", to moments of *de-synchronization*, when one is out of phase. When conditions are favourable, interaction leads to the acquisition of a better relational competence – at first implicit, but then later also explicit. Abstract meanings are also always at stake: *directly* when linguistic abilities are shared; *indirectly* when only one of the actors involved has such abilities.

Starting from the premise that I would be utterly incapable of giving up either one or the other, and that they enrich each other splendidly, in essence, the way Bion depicts the mother–child relationship (as seen above, more as a theorist than as a "paediatrician") ultimately has many more concrete and innovative technical repercussions on the way we work. To put it in a nutshell, with Winnicott you can still work in the mainstream, whereas with Bion you are forced to choose. He changes all the known coordinates of the theoretical scene and sets in motion a strikingly new approach.

Note

1   https://www.youtube.com/watch?v=GXp_KROm-V0

Chapter 4

How does it cure?

In this chapter I will discuss in more detail the main tools that analysts use in their clinical work when treating patients. The idea of the toolbox tells us a lot about analytic field theory. Bion made a superlative contribution to psychoanalysis, but many authors who are inspired by his thinking remain to a greater or lesser extent confined within the Kleinian framework. It is only thanks to the coming together in BFT of the various trends and authors I have examined in earlier chapters that we have come to build up a true toolbox. By "tools" I mean concepts and theories that are not too ambiguous, are easy to pass on to others, and that are able to open up a new way of working, one that is alive and in accord with contemporary epistemology.

Interpretation or conversation?

Since it is important to understand whether the emotional atmosphere of the analytic field is conducive or not to the forging of bonds, that is, to psychic growth – growth which, according to Bion, takes place when the "truth" that is the food of the mind is generated – it becomes important to use all the tools that enable us to get in touch with this climate. Only then can we try to tell whether it is L ("bullish") or H ("bearish"). Below I describe this task as intuiting the "waking dream thought" of the analytic field in order to *become*, as it were, the O of the session.

When the analytic field is in a regressive mode (in H), the analyst faces the problem of how to get it back to being progressive

DOI: 10.4324/9781003219972-4

(in L). More often than not, this involves conversing with the patient in a way that makes them feel acknowledged. I have schematized for educational and exercise purposes some of the possibilities available to the analyst using an acronym: SCREAM.

This approach implies that for me the moment (a) of *interpretation* marks above all the analyst's receptivity to what is happening on the unconscious level of the relationship, while the moment (b) of *conversation* is the term I use to refer to the analyst's conscious interventions designed to steer the analytic process in the direction of cure.

In short, for the purposes of *recognition*, emotional attunement (the development of the psychic container) comes before or is more important than intellectual agreement (the identification of psychic content).

These are the main tools for trying to guess what the quality of the bond or the analytical field is at a given time: dreams, reveries, action reveries, somatic reveries, dream flashes, transformation in dream and transformation in hallucinosis.

Dream

Dreams continue to be the extraordinary gateway to the unconscious they have always been. Recounting a dream is always in itself a highly significant gesture of willingness to engage in an intimate relationship and to play the game of interpretation. Moreover, it is an indication that a more than adequate ability to symbolize is already present.

In BFT, however, the analyst listens to the patient's dream narrative (or her own, i.e., the dream that within another theoretical framework would be called a countertransference dream) as if it were the dream of the analytic field dreamt in the here and now, that is, the *joint* dream that the third mind of analyst and patient dreams in real time about itself.

In other words, the analyst does not listen to the dream by objectifying it as if it were only the dream the patient had at night and the *via regia* to *his* psyche, and she does not listen to the dream in the manner of an account of the night-time or current dream as exclusive to the patient (or, when it happens, to herself).

To take a schematic example: *A., a patient, says he dreamt of a lion in the garden and ran into the house to hide.* From a field perspective this would mean: *we are dreaming that a lion is roaming free in the garden and we have barricaded ourselves in the house*; or today we feel (or it feels) like we are in a situation where we are terrified of being attacked and mauled by a wild beast.[1] Clearly a possible first hypothesis is that the emotional atmosphere of the field is truly steeped in persecution (H), and that sooner rather than later something must be done to make it livable once again.

Reverie

A reverie is a dream we have while we are awake. It happens all the time; it is like the breathing of the mind, but we do not usually pay attention to it. If we do pay attention to it, we treat it exactly like the story of a night-time dream or like the story of an event in reality – but fictionalized, that is to say, transformed into a dream. Like a nocturnal dream, a reverie always has a special status because it puts us more directly in touch with the transformative work performed by the alpha function. Instant after instant it has to digest beta elements and produce alpha elements. Subsequently, these become part of the construction of both dream and waking thoughts.

The question of what *to do* technically with a reverie is no different from what to do with a dream or, in other models, a countertransference dream. There is never a simple answer because each concept represents a node in a network of concepts. Could it ever be argued that a classical interpretation rests on a more secure basis than the interpretation or "field use" of a reverie? I don't think so. There is an equal likelihood of it being used properly or being misused.

Having said that, I repeat: essentially the analyst would use the reverie in the same way as the dream in the previous example. It does not matter if it is told by the patient (seen simply as the person who accepts the task of "reading" the text that has been written together) or if it came to her mind. For example, at one point she may have thought of a news story from years earlier in which a tiger killed the woman who was feeding it that day at the zoo but who had been careless and left a small door open in the cage. Unlike associations, reveries present themselves, just like dreams, without a recognizable link to the analytic dialogue; they are received in a state of passivity, delve deeper and expresses directly the unconscious emotion in the form of stories and images.

Action reverie and somatic reverie

It seems to me that in psychoanalysis all the time we have to deal with two big issues, two splits. In a significant quote, Ludwig Binswanger (Spiegelberg, 1972, p. 202), the founder of existential psychology, says that the split between subject and object (which comes primarily from Descartes) is "the cancer of psychology". The other split is between mind and body. We won't get very far if we simply privilege the body over the mind. The point is to think of them not in terms of a dichotomy but rather in dialectical terms. It should be obvious to us that we are immersed in the world and that we generate meaning through our body (sensations, emotions, actions), and that, at the same time, as Heidegger (1987, p. 249) writes, "receiving-perceiving is always language and jointly a saying of words". That is why conceptualizing the place of the body in analysis is of the utmost importance.

Let us now address somatic reverie or what, in homage to action painting (also known as "gestural abstraction"), I have come to call *action reverie*. In my eyes, and in line with what I have been arguing, in general the semiotic processes of signification cannot be separated from the semantic processes of signification – incidentally, even the word has a body, and especially the poetic word. So, if it has any specific meaning, in analogy with the concerns and affectivity of the hypochondriac, action reverie would involve drawing attention to non-verbal communication. Sensations, gestures, but also prolonged sequences of interaction, for example in communication using cell phone apps, etc., can be interpreted as field phenomena.

The difference between action reverie and somatic reverie is that the former consists primarily in actions, while the latter is made up of bodily sensations of various kinds.

Dream flashes

We use the term dream flashes to refer to images with a strong sensory component that suddenly impose themselves on the analyst's mind, similarly to a dream or a reverie consisting of a single hyperinflated image, a bit like the memories which Freud calls "hyperluminous" (*überdeutlich*) and to which he attributes a special meaning. On the level of interpretation, we would treat them no differently from any other psychic production on the dream spectrum. If a patient who has just been asked to pay a higher fee exclaims that the poster for *Psycho* has suddenly appeared before his eyes (with an almost hallucinatory vividness that he more than anyone else finds surprising), it would be enough to assume that at that moment the quality of the emotional bond for *both* of them is intensely persecutory.

Transformation in dream

Transformation in dream (TD) is one of the most valuable tools we have at our disposal to be able to apprehend the dream dimension of the analytic session. The central idea is that what is said in analysis can be heard as if it were the interweaving of narrative derivatives coming from waking dream thought. A simple technical device is to preface what the patient says (or even what the analyst says, since in this model both are "places" in the analytic field) with the short phrase: "*I dreamt that…*" or "*I am dreaming that…*", or better still "*We are dreaming that…*". In this way, by using this ingenious device – a shuttle moving between different symbolic worlds – we immediately re-contact the unconscious level of communication and are able to restore the quality of the emotional experience at hand. It is a simple and intuitive way of tuning into the unconscious (dreamlike) flow of the dialogue; another simile might be to compare it to the devices that make it possible to switch between the railway tracks. The reality recounted by the patient, which is often two-dimensional, immediately regains the vividness and full dimension of the dream. *Ferro's great merit is that he not only clearly formulated this concept but also radicalized it in a very original way and in absolute logical coherence with the theory – and this is what makes BFT truly unique*. We can safely say that after the invention of the concept of transformation in dream, and moreover remaining faithful to the spirit, if not the letter, of Freud, BFT brings to completion the paradigm shift in psychoanalysis that we have already attributed to Bion.

It is essential to bear in mind that in our work it would be absurd to put too much emphasis on transforming in dreams – in other words, relentlessly interpreting the unconscious texture of reality. We would find ourselves leaning too heavily towards the rational and abstract pole of thinking, and overly limiting our oneiric or imaginative capacity and our involvement in the relationship. To avoid falling into a mechanical use of TD, it is best that the analyst should internalize it first, forget it and then rediscover it each time, or better, *let herself be rediscovered by it*. A feeling of *surprise* will often be the sign that a radical reversal of perspective has taken place. This is a crucial point. The difference between the two ways of listening is the same as that between voluntary and involuntary memory. The ideal use of transformation in dreams is paired with the state of passivity that Bion recommends and indeed prescribes in the form of the concept of negative capability/faith (NC/F), that is, listening without memory, without desire and without understanding, and the switching between that and the selected fact (NC/F↔SE).

In some cases, the analyst can break this rule and use TD to "force" the dream in the session. She may even resort to it intentionally in less inspired moments to unblock a situation of aridity and desperate repetitiveness. Even if used in a more active way, and not according to the passivity of NC/F (which is after all a different kind of activity), the result is always a kind of enchanting magic.

The character as a narrative hologram of the session and emotional function

One of the easiest ways to transform the concreteness of material reality into a dream is to pay attention to the "characters" and narrative plots that develop in the analytic dialogue. The analyst deduces the H or L quality of the function from the actions of the characters. Each character can be considered as a kind of *field hologram*, that is to say, an emotional or affective or bonding *function* that is active at any given time. As in the case of holograms, which form at the intersection of two distinct beams of projection, but then merge in it and are no longer separable, it is difficult to tell whether it belongs to the patient or to the analyst. In actual fact, it belongs to the field they bring to life by virtue of their closeness and the fact that they are involved with each other and already endowed with "valences".

This is the term Bion uses for the disposition human beings possess to communicate in a non-verbal way and also to influence each other unconsciously. It is the same phenomenon that prompts Freud to speak of communication from unconscious to unconscious, and that neuroscientists explain by highlighting its biological bases, for example, mirror neurons.

Models for the concept of field-characters are *Six Characters in Search of an Author* and *Tonight We Improvise*, both by Pirandello; then, Vladimir Propp's famous study (1928) on the morphology of the fairy tale, which had so much influence on structuralism, and whose central thesis is that there is an infinite number of characters but only a limited number of narrative functions. "Characters" can of course be not only human beings or animals, etc., but also abstract entities. Often these are *secondary characters* that at a certain point become protagonists or *hidden characters* that come to light only thanks to the perception of formal aspects of the analytic discourse or as a result of events like parapraxes (especially if interpreted as transformations in hallucinosis).

Transformation in hallucinosis

The concept of transformation in hallucinosis (TH) had its origin in Bion but only became a proper technical tool as part of BFT. In short, TH, based on Bion's two new postulates of the unconscious and the dream, overturns the classical interpretation of errors, slips in speech and actings-out. These are no longer clues that disclose the secret (and often "evil") impulses of the patient's (or, possibly, the analyst's) unconscious. On the contrary, the analyst reads them as forms of joint creation of meaning. Unlike TD, TH becomes such only when the analyst realizes the "error" (a second later, or months later) and rectifies it, in the same way as we wake up from a dream. Literally, much more than reverie or the recounting of a dream, TH *is* a dream made in a state of wakefulness.

The term "hallucinosis" is therefore only a metaphor derived from its specific use in psychiatric semeiotics to express the idea that a subject can be in the grip of a dreamlike (hallucinatory) activity without actually being asleep (in the original meaning: without personality deterioration; or, being able to realize and criticize his misperceptions). Basically, TH is merely a special case of the normal hallucinatory activity that physiologically infiltrates perception. Its distinctive feature is the *intensity* that goes so far as to produce a distortion of reality. However, we do not see this distortion in the same way as Freud's idea of dream distortion, which has the meaning of hiding something that is located "behind". Quite the opposite, we see it as a form of expression that signals a particular emotional *urgency*.

Perhaps these "hallucinations" occur when we are more prey to the anxiety we feel at not being able to understand or make sense of things. A situation is then created in which it is as if in the process of the emotional digestion of raw sensations, projective activity comes to prevail over perceptual activity, thus rendering visible a presence that normally goes unnoticed. As long as we are inside the "hallucination", we can do nothing about it. But if and when we realize that we are mistaken, then the hallucinosis or lucid "hallucination" turns into dreaming (*dreaming means not only immersing oneself in the hallucinations of the dream but also waking up*). At that point a symbolic form becomes available to us, equivalent in all respects to night-time dreams, which we can use to try to reconnect with the patient. Terror at loss of meaning – at losing the internalized object that orientates us in the world – is reversed into the sublime experience of an epiphany of meaning.

Literally implying a waking dream, TH is the technical tool that – as the psychic faculty most capable of thinking about infinity – makes the unconscious work harder. This is why TH has the vividness and force of a conviction that only dreams have while we are dreaming them, and again immediately after we have awoken and are still under the spell of their images.

So, we no longer look at dreams with suspicion and view their images as unacknowledged representations that have temporarily eluded repression, but rather as expressions of the unceasing work done by the unconscious to make "poetic" sense of reality. TH is in line with the "scandalous" principle formulated by Ferro that it may sometimes make more sense to speak before thinking rather than the other way round. The reason is obvious: this can be a way of making the unconscious speak and of activating its function of symbolization, which is mostly achieved by adopting the principles of negative capability and the unconscious as a psychoanalytic function of personality.

What then is the difference between TD and TH? The difference is that, as with reverie, TD is mostly *conscious* and *intentional*. In TD I "decide" to listen in a certain way. In reverie, images cross my mind but I still "know" that I am awake and that they are fantasy images. This is not the case with TH. As we said, until I rectify the "error" (an "awakening" that happens immediately in the form of slips and parapraxes, but that can take much longer in many other cases, when it is of a different nature), *I am absolutely convinced of it*. It is as if I were completely immersed in the phantasmagoria of dream images. If I did not wake up from the dream, I would not know that I had "dreamt". It is only when I come to realize my "hallucination" that I turn it into a "hallucinosis". While the pattern does in some way follow that of TD or of reverie, significantly different degrees of awareness are implied.

Conversation as a path to recognition

Another way of paying attention to non-verbal communication – ideally, always understood as joint dreaming – is to try as hard as possible to make the interpretation natural[2] or embodied. To take a small example of the concept of embodiment that everyone can understand: in the past if I had to delete a document from my computer screen, computers with other operating systems asked me to type strings of instructions. Instead my Mac allowed me to simply drag it into the trash. It is clear that the second method is more immersive and spontaneous. With virtual reality, nowadays, you do not press buttons or type strings of instructions but just wear gloves and move your hands. This means that the instructions are more and more embodied. So there is increasingly less of a distinction between *immersion* and *interactivity* (Civitarese, 2008).

My idea is that the same should happen with interpretation as the equivalent of "giving instructions", i.e., "interpreting", in the virtual/dream reality or space of the analytic setting. It should be natural, unsaturated and discursive. We should participate in the dialogue with spontaneity and aliveness, without interrupting "the movie" (the emotion) or the narrative. Immersion should always be guided by interpretation and interpretation should always be in some way immersive. Interpretation might be a bit more immersive or a bit more interactive. This is the opposite of telling the patient: "What you are telling me is something completely different from what you think".

Analysis, to me, is more of a conversation than a question of giving interpretations. No matter what narrative register the patient is using (dream, memory, fantasy, perception), *the aim is always to gather clues to intuit how the process of mutual recognition is unfolding*. Here, by "interpretation" I mean what you actually say to the patient, but I also mean how the analyst listens to the unconscious in the analytic dialogue. The two moments are linked, but the former (interpretation as listening) remains implicit (I*i*), while the latter (interpretation as a certain type of comprehension offered to the patient) becomes explicit (I*e*). But the key point is that it should be obvious to us that *both somehow have powerful effects on the analytic field.* In a way, both are "interpretations". A silent interpretation can affect the analytic field far more powerfully than a verbalized interpretation. The reason is that it changes the emotional tone (*Stimmung*) of the field.

Thus *interpretation* (of the unconscious) *and recognition* become the two key words in our work – the alpha and omega of clinical practice. What we aim for is *recognition*. The thing is that mutual recognition is not just *conscious* recognition. Thinking of it as just conscious is a common mistake. Recognition is a label for the process whereby a mind is born and grows. Why do we interpret the unconscious? Because we are trying to get an idea of how this process is going forward, whether in the right or the wrong direction, and whether it is progressive or regressive. All psychoanalysis can be summarized in these two words: *interpretation* and *recognition*. An immersive interpretation is an interpretation that no longer comes with a label attached to it that reads "interpretation".

Interpretation is mainly about the way of listening (I*i*) to the discourse of the unconscious.

Unsaturated interpretation and the SCREAM acronym

Whatever intervention (I*e*) the analyst offers it is important that it stems from I*i*, or from her receptivity to the *Ucs*. People always ask me what I tend to say to the patient. In the end, I decided to invent an acronym to sum up the spectrum of possible things to say: SCREAM: offer Self-disclosure (rarely and with caution), play the Greek Chorus, pay attention to Reveries, map the Emotion, make sure not to miss transformations in hAllucinosis (the Italian word is "allucinosi"), reformulate with a Metaphor or a simile what the patient has just said, etc.

But the analyst can also offer "deep" interpretation *if* this is a language that can be shared with the patient and still be using a "language of achievement", as Bion names it. Still, the key factor in therapy is the analyst's receptivity to the discourse of the unconscious. It is the quality of her listening, *how* she listens in order to get onto the patient's emotional wavelength.

If while listening I maintain the *you* and *I split*, then it is all about "You are doing this to me", "I am doing this to you", "You are unconsciously attacking, seducing, manipulating, resisting...", or, it is me doing the same. Instead, if I listen from a field point of view, I see whatever is said as the reflection of what *we* are dreaming together. *This is a catastrophic change*: as I said earlier, I go from seeing the profiles in Edgar Rubin's famous ambiguous or bi-stable figure to seeing the vase. In the same way, it is not that, if we focus on the unconscious functioning of the couple in the here and now, the individual history and the actual trauma will disappear. *If I concentrate for a while on the vase, the profiles are still there.* But if I listen from this perspective, whatever I say to the patient sounds different. It is also an interpretation that most of the time sticks within the narrative genre proposed by the patient. In other words, the primary goal is to develop tools for thinking. Finding meaningful content is useful, but the main thing is to respect the patient's ability to tolerate what we tell him or her. Content that outstrips the capacity of the container risks being iatrogenic. Both content and container are important, but *hierarchically the latter comes first*.

If we are watching a film we find fascinating (for example, *The Last of the Mohicans*, a film I am very fond of and have seen multiple times), and at a certain point someone interrupts the movie and calls upon a critic to explain it, we would be very annoyed. Things are different in the case of the character of critic in Fellini's *8½* (in my opinion, his most beautiful movie), or also through the protagonist in Levenson's *Malcom & Marie*. Fellini and Levenson are masters of dreams; they do not break up the story.

Another example: Paula tells the analyst that her mother used to be able to freeze her movements with a single glance. She had trained her to respond instantly to the slightest nod. An analyst might say that there is someone here who seems to demand absolute control, and who grants the other little freedom to move as she wishes. The message between the lines is: "This could be you seeing me as a 'Medusa analyst' who turns you to stone with a glance. But it's your misunderstanding, and the explanation lies in your past history – this is who you are". In this way, the analyst shifts the scene from the patient's story, which was about the past.

This is why elsewhere (Civitarese, 2008) I have talked about transference interpretation as the rhetorical figure of *metalepsis*, or the breach of the temporal frame of the story. For example, at the end of a short story by Cortázar the main character stabs the reader. There are other examples in Woody Allen's movies. An immersive commentary that respected the narrative plan proposed by the patient, and that also aimed to be interactive (in other words, sought to produce positive "climatic" changes), would come from an interpretation of what is going on that more often than not the analyst keeps in his mind. It could simply be: "She [the mother] struck you with a look" (in Italian "struck" is "fulminava", and "fulmine" is *lightning*, so I am also using a metaphor). Another comment could be: "This would be like living in barracks"; or: "In situations like this you are terrified of making mistakes".

So, again, the most important thing is *how* you listen. Mostly it is better to respect the patient's narrative frame, and just to comment on the story she is telling, but the analyst listens in terms of *we-ness* in the here and now. In the vignette, there seems to be a certain "inhibition" in the air, this fear (*your* fear/*my* fear), that someone says something and this Medusa-like gaze might make an appearance. As an example: if I then just make a generic comment about what happened in the past, and if from a theoretical angle I listen as if anything said or felt unconsciously is always about what is going on, this would be a way of taking responsibility for what *is* truly happening.

The analyst sets past history to one side so as to focus on how the analytic dialogue, no matter what it is ostensibly about, actually reflects the emotional linking or function that is active in the here and now. In this case, the air is pervaded by the terror of being hurt by a chilling, mortifying look. It is something that arises from the common unconscious level of two minds that communicate with each other and form a field system. This is why we speak of field – "field" is just a metaphor. There is this layer that we conceptualize as a shared indistinct layer – inevitably we use spatial metaphors, but it would be better to talk about *processes* – where we could not say "This is yours, this is mine".

It is then up to the analyst, as a separate subject, to take responsibility for facilitating positive transformations. This is what she does. The barber cuts his client's hair, the analyst aims to get in touch with her patient. However, she knows that, inevitably, she will never have total control over what she decides to do. Again, this means that we should always listen for signals from the intersubjective third or field. We need to listen to how (unconsciously, together) we try to transform the new *beta*-signals that continuously impinge upon the field. The process never stops.

The concept of classical psychoanalysis that comes closest to this is interpretation, not *of* transference, but *in* the transference. The difference is obvious, because, if we speak of interpretation *in* the transference, the frame is still that of the patient who distorts or misrepresents the analyst. It would then be a mistake to say that unsaturated interpretation is the same as interpretation in the transference. The conceptual and theoretical frame is completely different. We can see two subjects either as interacting or as forming a third mind (field, or system), something more than just interaction. For all these reasons, there can be no external criterion that helps us find a perfect balance between immersion and interpretation. In my opinion, the balance is found by developing one's own sensitivity to a radical oneiric perspective in the session and to the unconscious discourse. Obviously, in this way the analyst can monitor the climate changes in the field, and also receive reports on her conscious moves.

I have to say that my reason for using the idea of immersion versus interactivity is also in order to clarify another point. Sometimes (in fact, *multiple* times), we are as it were "lost" in the naïve realism of everyday life. This is not something we need to bother too much about; the important thing is to understand the concept of the shared dream of the session. Sooner or later, with surprise and gratitude for the method, this principle will come back to us. As James Grotstein (2007) used to say, you do not have to worry about listening without memory and desire. Memory, desire and comprehension will come back to you at the right time. They will awaken you from being stuck to reality or concreteness and will bring you back to our concept of inter-activity, or *immersive interactivity* (which is different from mere immersion) – this is the moment when we "interpret".

Regrettably, it seems that Ferro and I, and other kindred authors, are unable to convey the idea that analysis, in our understanding of it, does not take place in a vague, dreamy, or unreal atmosphere. Sometimes we give this impression, because we put too much emphasis on the idea of dreaming the session. But this notion just serves as a reminder that to some extent we always need to be woken up by or at least to listen to the shared uncon-scious meaning of whatever is being said. Nothing more.

For example, if the patient's proposed narrative register is that of history, or the trauma of current reality, we obviously respect this domain of discourse. To take a banal example, if a patient says, "Yesterday the cat ran out of the house", I might simply ask, "Why did that happen?" Patient: "Because someone stupidly left the door open". I could say, "Sometimes we think we can trust someone in the family, but then we realize it would have been better not to". So, you see, that's very open. But in my mind, I am taking responsibility for this – we left some "door" open, and the "cat" ran out. And the patient could say, "Yes, but usually they are careful". This could be a sign that the patient felt contained by my comment. I may say, "True", and immediately we enter a less persecutory atmosphere. "What would we do if we couldn't trust anyone in the house?" The patient might say, "But now, I do not know where the cat is, and I am very worried". I could reply, "Yes, because you would imagine that it might get into some kind of trouble". The patient: "Yes, but cats are said to have nine lives", and so on.

What I'm *not* going to say is something like "You're telling me that we're having a dream in which a cat ran out of the house because someone left the door open; that dream is a kind of a reverie that tells us what happens to us when we are immersed in a climate of worry, anxiety and mutual distrust; it is true that we seem to think we have sufficient resources to solve it". By no means am I going to say that. I remain on the level of the patient's discourse, but I *listen*. What is important is that if I listen in a certain way, I *trust* my unconscious and the patient's unconscious, and I stop being suspicious or moralistic. In fact, *inevitably*, even if I listen in this way, I get to know everything about the patient's life, the patient's past, the trauma he has suffered – I don't see any problem with that. I see no difficulty in maintaining this kind of binocular vision, which, as with eyesight, lends depth and perspective. On the other hand, this kind of functional split or creative dissociation between different planes of intentionality is normally used in everyday life when we speak on the level of allusion, or use irony, or read a fairy tale, etc. Still, I have to admit that we do not seem to be able to clarify this question effectively to colleagues through the clinical examples we describe.

The shift from *I/you* to *we* and the ethics of psychoanalysis

A., a patient, recounts that he had already tried psychotherapy but that he stopped a short time later because he felt constantly *ashamed* and *judged* by the therapist. There was, he says, *intolerable pressure*. The analyst can listen in a variety of ways:

I

In a first model, the analyst discusses with him the content of his discourse, making clever observations about the emotion involved and reactions. She links cause and effect but always remains on a concrete or realistic level. To simplify somewhat, we could see this way of working as doing "just" PSYCHOTHERAPY.

II

In a second model, the analyst hypothesizes that if the patient feels judged and ashamed it is because he is projecting onto her the unconscious image (*imago*) of a strict parent, in other words, he is making a transference. However, she might also think that she is really unconsciously putting too much pressure on A. She would then think either of her own transference on him or of a response to his transference, that is to say, a countertransference effect. In this way of working we would recognize the cornerstones of the CLASSICAL FREUDIAN MODEL of working.

III

Taking a third case, the analyst might think that A. is putting pressure on her and somehow making her act in a certain way. *He* is the one who is putting pressure on the therapist. He would be trying to get rid of a certain psychic content that he cannot tolerate any more and project it into her.

It looks like a kind of *transference+++* based not on infantile neurosis but on unconscious primitive fantasies activated in the here and now. This would place us within a KLEINIAN MODEL.

IV

Another example could take inspiration from the RELATIONAL or INTERPERSONAL MODEL: the analyst realizes that for two months (or whatever period of time) she has *actually* been putting a lot of pressure on A. She would interpret this fact as part of yet another rendition of a childhood scene in which he was treated this way by his mother, and would consider that she was enticed by the patient into an enactment, i.e., playing the role of the mother.

V

From the point of view of BFT, the analyst would think that after choosing the characters of "patient" and "psychotherapist" for the story they are writing together (or dream they are dreaming, or game they are playing), they are, in the here and now, trying to make sense of and give meaning to the *proto-sensoriality* that arises in the field. *This specific narrative of the interrupted therapy is the product of their shared unconscious work*. She would see this activity as the best they have been able to achieve in this particular session. The emotion that is reflected in the story (dream or game) that they have unconsciously and consciously created together is *the O of the session*, that is, *the basic assumption of the group* of two that they form. Then she would ask herself: *Is it H or L? Does it promote growth or does it destroy links?* Since in their case it is about *shame* and *fear* of judgement, the narrative seems to indicate that there is an increase in the cruelty of critical consciousness (Super-ego) which causes pain in both of them. There is always a basic reciprocity: they both unconsciously feel pressured by judgement and feel ashamed at not living up to each other's expectations. Of course, by "narrative" we mean not just words but, as already explained, feelings, emotions, sensations, reveries, actions, etc.

Compared to the other models, two very important consequences flow from being receptive to the discourse of the unconscious:

A. I TRUST the patient and myself: I STOP LISTENING SUSPICIOUSLY according to a conception of the unconscious as hell (resistance, manipulation, seduction, etc.).

B. The story is about US, *you&me*, not just you *or* me. I INEVITABLY FEEL MORE INVOLVED, MORE ALIVE AND MORE RESPONSIBLE. *What is close to us matters most.*

C. I come into closer contact with my own feeling of shame and am in a better position to deal with it; in other words, I see the inevitable REVERSIBILITY implied in any field emotion/affect. This is why it can be said that *even an emotion of which either the patient or the analyst is aware remains unconscious until it is located in the field and is attributed to both actors.* It is not enough to say that patient and analyst are "places" in the field, as the metaphor of the field serves precisely to establish an angle of vision from which, on the unconscious level, no "place" is distinct from another.

On a more general level, I think that this kind of listening gives us the chance to free psychoanalysis as much as possible from the dross of ideology and "arrogance" that can easily infiltrate it, and therefore the chance to achieve its ethical re-foundation.

Notes

1 The basic technique of analysis is on the one hand to deconcretize reality and on the other to concretize dreams. If I want to have an idea of the unconscious climate that pervades the analytic field or the internal world of the patient, or my own, I have to think about what I would feel *if* I really met a lion in the garden.

2 Mitchell Wilson (2020) reminds us that Jacob Arlow used to say that the analyst should talk to patients the same way she might talk to a taxi driver.

Chapter 5

Clinical examples

BFT radically embraces Bion's basic principles, but also complements them with various original concepts. Above all, it adds a theory of technique that is versatile in its clinical application and easy to pass on. In my opinion, this is what makes Bion's ideas truly serviceable nowadays and can protect us, as Ferro writes, from the not always rigorous use – a kind of *Bion à la carte* – that some make of its key postulates. In particular, I would like to emphasize the precept of considering the *whole* session, and in the supervision session also the anamnestic account, as a dream – the place, according to Meltzer (1984), where meaning is generated; in other words, more precisely, the fact of paying attention to all the manifestations of the oneiric spectrum; and also the idea of letting oneself be guided by the interplay of the characters. The theoretical-technical devices illustrated in the following vignettes are not to be found in Bion as such but are to be considered a creative development of his theories. However, the very valuable concept of negative capability/faith should be kept in mind.

In order to illustrate the various examples, I will use some short analysis or supervision vignettes for reasons of confidentiality. As with analysis, my understanding and practice of supervision involves more than just giving guidance on matters of theory and technique. On the contrary, it is also a way of engaging with the supervisee in a shared unconscious work to give emotional-experiential meaning to the way the supervision session itself unfolds, and, by reflection, to the original one between patient and analyst. The aim is to get to the point of "dreaming" the problem that is at the heart of the

DOI: 10.4324/9781003219972-5

"nightmare" that analyst and patient are experiencing. In the analytic session, the unconscious emotional experience of the couple is inferred from the analytic dialogue during the session; in supervision, the text to be considered is already written, but reading it together in a new context also means rewriting it. In both cases it is a matter of activating an "integrated" mode of listening that is both logical and affective; it involves, as it were, letting the intersubjective (joint) unconscious function of both patient and analyst characters (or of the field) do its work. I hope that these vignettes can give a rough idea of the new interpretative possibilities afforded by BFT, relying on the concept of transformation as opposed to distortion.

As we well know, one can easily spend hours on two lines of text, and this is what accounts for much of the charm of psychoanalysis and the game of interpretation. So I will limit myself here to giving very brief examples of how the analyst can listen to the text of the session or supervision using a field frame. At all events, what should be evident is the transition from a kind of work that is based on the concept of distortion to one based on the concept of transformation. The former focuses on the reconstruction of the past and on linking trauma to transference, and therefore on the patient's misunderstandings. The latter, while it also in some way and *inevitably* explores the patient's past and present, focuses in particular on the quantum level of constructing tools for thinking in the here and now.

What we see in all these examples is how we can work by having a coherent and rigorous (radical) notion of the meaning of the communication between minds that takes place at the unconscious level. We can safely say that it reflects the most extreme way at the same time as representing the state of *openness* or mutual influence between individuals. Referring to this capacity, Freud (1921, p. 107) speaks of "contagion" (*Infektion*), Bion (1961) of "valences", as in chemistry, and Hegel (1807, p. 295), paradoxically, since it implies a process leading to self-consciousness, of "infection" (*Ansteckung*).

Transformation in hallucinosis and hidden characters

Concreteness

A colleague has prepared a written text for a supervision. She asks me to skip the first page of the patient's life story and start directly from page two. In the session she reports in indirect speech practically only what the patient is talking about: a long list of bereavements and traumas. From a field perspective, this does not only concern the session itself but broadens to include the supervision session. It immediately occurs to me who/what might be the most important "character" in the session: its concreteness, and therefore also the concreteness of the analyst's listening. The session, which is read aloud, usurps the place usually reserved for the anamnesis, which *was not* read. In this way, it takes on the same factual character of past history and material reality. The exchange suggests a kind of (temporary?) deafness to what is going on in the analytic field in the here and now.

What I am implying is that this kind of action reverie already anticipates that the analyst tends to read the analytic dialogue without transforming it in dream; that is, without asking herself what its unconscious meaning might be. Instead, she reads it as mere fact, as one normally does with the anamnestic part. This is then confirmed when the text is actually read out during the session. At this point, it would not be absurd to see the climate of mourning that pervades the whole session – caused by the presence of several traumatic memories – as a metaphor/dream of loss of contact between analyst and patient.

This is an example of how a completely marginal event can be made significant as a way of restoring a sufficient level of emotional attunement. The underlying theoretical assumption is to see it as that which is dreamt by a field alpha function that comes into play both in the session with the patient and in the supervision. Note then the paradoxical nature of the gesture of recommending that I skip the first page of the text. It both expresses a suggestion to put aside history and concreteness – Bion would talk about listening without trying to remember anything – and diagnoses with extreme precision that it is something that is *not* happening at the moment when the place where we normally find the anamnesis is substituted by the text of the analytic conversation. A kind of split seems to have occurred between theory and practice, a split that the field is unconsciously trying to repair through an action reverie.

Laura or Mario?

Laura tells the analyst she is upset that Mario did not invite her to his party. The analyst speculates that Mario may not have invited her because she always tends to decline such invitations. In this way, she justifies him. I hypothesize that Laura may have felt that she was being reflected in a mirror that reveals to her that she has a stain on her dress, that she does not deserve to be invited, or that there is something wrong with her. At a certain point, however, I mistakenly say Mario instead of Laura. I then think, to my surprise, that it is as if I (or rather, the "we" that speaks through the patient or even through myself) had unconsciously recognized that, on the whole, the analyst had really succeeded in taking on Laura's point of view; that is to say, she justified not Mario but Laura-as-Mario, and shared her fear that others would laugh at her. My (our) unconscious reading somehow corrects my (our) conscious reading

Naomi Campbell

P: I'm learning to forgive. My best friend, Giada, slept with my boyfriend. I laugh about it now. In that case, the betrayal was twofold. I want to confront her, not play the game of silence. I confessed my insecurity. Maybe he's content to be with me. I'm not Naomi Campbell, maybe he would like a woman like her? She has nice long legs and a nice a…

A: Of course, knowing you are Naomi Campbell can be painful, but you must have other qualities inside you.

Actually the analyst meant that knowing she is NOT Naomi Campbell can be painful. As always, the mistake reveals another possible truth: is it not possible that it is painful *to be* like the famous model, perhaps because she is only (or mainly) admired for her beauty? Or because, being black, she is part of a minority that has been and still is marginalized in numerous ways?

This is an example of how using TH can open up new perspectives of meaning. Of course, from a field perspective, at stake is the authenticity of the bond between patient and analyst and the related risks of 'betrayal'.

Spacings

The peculiarity of this particular text submitted for supervision is that it makes an utterly idiosyncratic use of ellipses. Sometimes simply the classic three dots, but elsewhere many more are added. Mostly the dots connect two words in the text ("feeling................................If I were") without there being a pause between them and the words themselves.

This is a list of all the occurrences I found on the last page of the text, *after removing all the words*:

......
....
....
....
....
....
....
....
....
,.................
....
....
....
....
....
....
....
....
....
....
......
....
....
....
....
....
....
....)..............
....
....

The following is what the same page would look like after greying out the words but keeping the position the ellipses occupy on the page:

sta a lei prendere spazio......)

E: eh io, diciamo sono sempre al solito punto.......le vacanze sono state tranquille....lo sai, io e il mi' marito non siamo di quelli che si discute, si fanno scenate................è stata una convivenza civile................D miracolosamente da un mese a questa parte sembra un altro bambino, non ha più fatto scenate, io a dire il vero sono anche preoccupata che possa esplodere da un momento all'altro, infatti spesso ci ho parlato, l'ho invitato a dirmi come si sentiva, se c'era qualcosa che non andava, ma lui mi ha detto che non voleva più comportarsi male.................chi lo sa forse davvero ha elaborato qualcosa dentro di se.............comunque lunedì rivede la S (la sua terapeuta) e vediamo...................in compenso adesso è il mezzano che fa confondere.........

Comunque devo riconoscere che il mi' marito effettivamente si è impegnato................ mi ha sostenuto di più con i bambini, spesso gli diceva di ascoltarmi quando magari li brontolavo e facevano finta di niente, gli diceva che facendo in un certo modo mi mancavano di rispetto.............in questo ha seguito quello che aveva detto la S...................................poi per il resto resta sempre lo stesso.........si è fatto prendere in giro da R per una settimana, gli diceva di fare i compiti dopo pranzo e R gli diceva che li avrebbe fatti la sera dopo la doccia, poi la sera gli diceva che li avrebbe fatti dopo cena.......io l'ho lasciato fare.......mi ero imposta di delegare a lui questa cosa.....................ma alla fine sono dovuta intervenire, non gli potevo permettere di prendere in giro in quel modo....l'ho messo a fare i compiti e da quel giorno li ha fatti sempre dopo pranzo insieme a D.........sarà un caso................... mah....................

.........Poi......con l'altro.........è andato via ad agosto arrabbiato perché non ero stata abbastanza presente, avevo sempre i bambini...................ci siamo sentiti, ci siamo sempre tenuti in contatto........un giorno mi dice che non è alla mia altezza, che ci dobbiamo separare perché io sto meglio dove sono, lui non potrebbe darmi niente.........e poi anche se io non lo cerco, è lui a ricercarmi e a dirmi che mi ama............ci siamo rivisti martedì mezz'ora per un saluto............(è laconica quando parla di lui, non scende in *particolari....)...........certo quello che provo per lui non lo provo per il mi' marito............*

................Se c'è una cosa che ho capito quest'estate, è che nonostante l'impegno che possa averci messo anche con i bambini, i miei sentimenti nei suoi confronti

The point here is to emphasize the amazing role played by a punctuation mark that enhances the text's strong visual impact. The lines made up of detached dots seem to allude to the regular breath of the relationship reflected in the rhythm of sessions (the "thing" or object is there) and separations (the "thing" or object is *not* there or is only symbolically present). Some of the lines of dots are tolerable and provoke thought (the *no-thing*, i.e. the symbol that stands for the thing); others are not and destroy it (*noughtness*), as when, in some cases, they almost seem to fall into a vacuum, as in the following example:

  "say...................."

In short, what stands out is this surprising representation of the affective metric of the relationship. Spacings become an important character in the story. The point I want to stress here is that it can be fruitful to look at the rhetoric used in the construction of the text as a way of dreaming the session.

Alan Turing

In another text presented for a group supervision, the analyst introduced the different sections using the following numbering and alignment on the pages:

  0000000000
  11111111111111111111
  2222222222222222222222
  33333333333333333
  4444444444444444444444444444

This detail did not go unnoticed. The patient, L., seemed to be jealously guarding a secret; or rather, a secret seemed to be contained in the text/analysis/field. The group interpreted the rows of numbers as a code that might unlock the key to the secret, like Alan Turing's brilliant deciphering of Enigma in the Second World War; this association already pointed to a certain persecutory feeling that was present but not known. The many zeros seemed to allude to Bion's *O* (the unconscious shared emotional experience) and to his "Dogsonian" mathematics, as he terms it in *Transformations*, after the author of *Alice in Wonderland*.

It goes without saying that the series of 3s in bold type (**3**s) recalled the centrality of the Oedipal triangulation. In short, the numbers are seen as "characters" in the analytic field and a representation of the path of subjectivation: the newborn (1) who meets the maternal function or *semiotic chora* provided by the mother (2) and then, already within her, the paternal/separating function (as reflecting the law), or so-called third (3). Obviously, the persecution in the analytic field might be related to "Oedipal" problems in the analyst's conscious management of emotional distance in the session.

In L.'s case, the diagnosis of breast cancer she had recently received could be read as an allegory about the field. The "breast cancer" or cancer of the object/analyst-as-"breast" could speak to the partial failure of the "sacred conversation" that essentially the analytic dialogue always represents.

Emoticon

The text of a session describes how the patient had started a relationship with a married woman after the analysis had begun, and at this point, possibly alluding to a so-called lateral transference,[1] the writer adds these punctuation marks:

(;;;)

Her intention was clearly to wink in a slightly smug and knowing way at her colleagues, as if to say: "But we know what this is all about!" Yet it was impossible, because of the obsessive repetitiveness, not to see these marks as hyperbole, or as a degradation of affect corresponding to the emoticon that is used to symbolize winking ;-).

When something like this happens, it is important to avoid immediately saturating it with various meanings. It is legitimate to ask: "Did the analyst and patient wink at each other? Did they experience a pleasant feeling of mutual understanding or was it something more like collusion?" But what matters more than answering these questions is that from that moment on the analyst has a *preconception* that may eventually come to be "realized" (as a fact) and become a thought. Now she has a kind of little receptacle that will consciously and unconsciously influence what she looks at and her choice of what to put in it.

Once placed in the box, the content called an analytic "fact" will acquire a certain synchronistic, *acausal ordered-ness*, in the sense that it cannot be based on the strict logic of cause and effect – which is what many of the material and non-material containers that we use actually do.

Thiamine

S. dreams that she is sitting in my waiting room and asks another patient what she should take to stop her hair falling out. "The only thing is thiamine!" is the obvious answer.

This is like saying that if you want to cure the sadness of separation in and between sessions, you don't necessarily need great Werther-like passions, all you need is some love (L), or a little *ti-am-ino* (in Italian "ti amo" means "I love you", and the suffix *-ino/a* has the function of a diminutive and usually also expresses intimacy, warmth and affection).

Bullying

A patient, R., says: "So, since 2008, after my divorce, I have felt guilty because I didn't want to be with my husband. The guilt was alive all the time. Then I ask the question... How did my mother interact *with me in my early years*? If she idealized me as a daughter and every time I failed to mirror that, she would be disappointed and show frustration. I think of the bullying period I went through in the early 1070s here at school in Milan. The impression I had was that I wouldn't fight back".

When reading the text ahead of a supervision, the analyst realizes that she made a mistake when writing because she did not insert "me" between "with" and "in". For the rest of the session, she adds, the patient continued to identify with her ("wanting to be me")!

The fragment of text lends itself to deconstruction and reconstruction using psychoanalytic theories as groups of transformation according to a chain of events of the type: The "me" is missing [*in this session, it is as if the analyst were absent and the patient felt not seen; more strictly speaking, from a field perspective, each of them felt not recognized by the other*]→I didn't mirror [*R. (each of them) feels somehow compelled to meet the analyst's (the other's) expectations*]→She would be disappointed and show frustration [*for both* of them *the air is steeped in persecution*]→ My bullying period [*the relationship is marked by a certain violence*] in the early 1070s [*another slip or transformation in hallucinosis: the date indicates the early Middle Ages: metaphorically something very ancient or a very primitive functioning*].

Untying the knot

C. My hope is fading... it is *a knot* impossible to untie, maybe we should cut it with a sword.

But I read "It is *not* impossible to untie". So I was on the verge of saying that *there was* hope because C. had said that "The knot was not impossible to untie". This sprang as it were from my dream before my 'awakening', before I realized my mistake. Even if the manifest content of what I had just thought and later did actually say is the same, that is, that there was hope, at that point the sentence pronounced only in my mind was not much more than a superficial, tentative or wishful comment. It is only when almost instantly and to my surprise I *did* wake up from the hallucinosis that I could feel this sentence as true. In fact, *this* is really what unconsciously they were telling themselves. But to make it visible, there needed to be an expansion of the field (and a third mind) in the supervision.

Happy ending

"Yes, a really good movie", comments L., and, he adds, "with a happy *and*ing". The detail that caught my attention was the spelling error. The unconscious is, however, never wrong. The *end* of the film of the session at that point could be seen as a request not to *end* it or as a happy goodbye. The word "end" had turned into the gerund of a verb derived from a particle that has the fundamental function of linking ("and"), a particle that does not separate but connects. Just like when children listen to a fairy tale and keep asking *"And* then? *and* then...?"

Action reverie

The enchanted castle

In several analyses we experience a situation like the one in *The Enchanted Castle*. Apparently, there is warmth, intimacy, fluidity, except that images and stories of very tragic events start to come out. However, they are not listened to using the tool that is the concept of the unconscious. Or, if they are, they are dismissed as "patient distortions" induced by transference.

During a Zoom session, out of shot the therapist puts her feet up on a stool to get a more comfortable and natural position. The gesture could be seen as a reverie in action or bodily reverie or as a transformation in action – as the dream of how it is possible for both of them to be freer and less constrained within rigid roles.

They had been having an argument about a session payment issue, but then an idyllic atmosphere returned. Now the analyst has the opportunity to get in touch with the mutual anger that still hovers in the air. In fact, despite the relaxed emotional climate that characterizes the session, reflected in the gesture of the feet, there is also the fact that one association we made was between "feet up" and *"Hands up! Your money or your life!"*.

The snail-tiger

An analyst tells me that at the beginning of the analysis she was afraid of her patient. To give me an idea of what this means, she tells me that she experienced her "as a snail". As she speaks, she mimes a gesture with her two hands as if she wanted to suggest a ferocious animal that is about to grab you and tear you apart. I am a bit surprised. When I was a kid, a play-mate and I used to organize snail races. It never occurred to me they were such dangerous animals. *"Maybe ... more of a tiger than a snail!"* I comment jokingly to my colleague.

We might think that such an aggressive snail – the dictionary defines it as a mollusc that belongs to the family of the pulmonate gastropods – possibly represented a threat to the narcissism of the analyst, who wanted more positive feedback about the efforts she was making in therapy and also *faster* progress. It is significant, however, that in Italian "mollusc" is a word that can be used about a person who is cowardly, inert, lacking in willpower and character.

The fact remains that this snail-tiger is an utterly memorable character; if we see it as a dreamlike symbol of analysis – but also of supervision – perhaps it embodies fear of exposing oneself to new ideas, of not being able to make them one's own, and thus seeming "slow" (not clever), etc. In short, new ideas experienced as tigers disguised as snails. From this angle, it would be legitimate to give the analyst's gesture the meaning of a shared *action reverie* that conveys an unconscious emotion that concerns both the patient when she is with the analyst, and vice versa, but also when she is with me in supervision. My approach then should be to scale down the vision from above (*super*) to such an extent that it can be tolerated. Essentially it is a sense of threat and therefore fear (red light) of the other's judgement. This is why the snail's two harmless *eye stalks* had turned into *claws*.

The cushion

Lori lies down on the couch but immediately turns around and looks at me with an expression of consternation on her face. "There's a piece missing!", she says. I then hand her the cushion that the previous patient has the habit of removing before each session and that I have not yet put back in its place. I explain to her what has happened, although I would have gladly not had to do so. After a pause I start trying to convince her again (it's almost as if I can't control myself). I tell her that in analysis small events like this are often significant. Habits develop and when something alters the routine people feel confused or disoriented. She asks: "Like falling, or feeling dizzy...!?" Once again, I catch myself saying something as if under duress, and I recall aloud the famous episode of the uneven pavement in the courtyard of a house in Paris that triggers in the narrator of Proust's *In Search of Lost Time* a series of involuntary memories about Venice. After a pause Lori says: "I was going to ask you about your interest in

Foucault. I saw that you have a biography of him, there on the shelf opposite". I ask her again if she has any ideas about this, and I think to myself what the connection might be with what we have just said. She: "Well, apart from his studies on madness, on the birth of the clinic.... For me... it's the homosexuality that interests me... A friend and I used to go to this club where we felt like objects of desire. It was an intoxicating feeling... There were trannies and lesbians... One time, I was menstruating and A. wanted to make love anyway. I saw all the blood and had the overwhelming feeling I needed to vomit, like when I fractured the base of my skull...". I tell her that I am struck by the analogy between the beginning of the session and this memory, that it has to do with another situation in which she felt lost... that there seems to be some connection between the two things. "Once, at school", she resumes, ""they put me on my own at a desk and the headmaster yelled at me that he was going to kick me out if I didn't stop disturbing them!"

When she arrives, Lori discovers that something is missing. The fact that it is a material object that allowed her to assume a certain body position, the context and the sense of dismayed surprise she expresses allow us to speculate that she might be reliving a sensory or semiotic trauma. An essential rhythm of being, related to analysis, seems to have been suddenly disrupted. We may think that it has something to do with a traumatic experience from the distant past inscribed in the unrepressed unconscious. That would explain why Lori reacts the way she does. As if she were lost. It should also be noted that I had forgotten to put the cushion back in its place. My failure to do this might concretely symbolize being deprived of the supportive and containing function of the analysis; it was as if I had felt it and needed to give it representability. Perhaps it served, as later happened, to prompt Lori to remember and perhaps to reconstruct the story behind an old wound.

The missing cushion had been her skull base fracture, the primordial trauma that had scarred her ability to think. The feeling of not having a place to rest one's head becomes the metalectic device that transports one from the scene of analysis into other orders of meaning: from the analytic field to the patient's internal world, and finally to her past. Could this in all cases be a lack of the maternal function of reverie? Could my act be seen as a kind of interpretation? Or as an enactment? In any case, it doesn't end there, because immediately afterwards I talk too much (as if activating a function of self-supervision) and I give her unnecessary explanations. Probably this happens because I was touched by the terror I saw glinting in her eyes and felt the need to repair the damage done. I felt I had to do or say something. In short, the impulse drove me to offer a cushion of words and a presence in addition to the actual cushion which I had already put back in place.

There is obviously a touch of intellectualization in my reference to Proust. On the one hand, feeling suddenly unbalanced, I take refuge in culture and books and distance myself from emotions that I feel are too oppressive; on the other, I remind myself that this is a writer I am really fond of, and not purely out of snobbery. So there is a sense of giving her something of mine that is also precious. As always, that is not the whole story: a few years ago I really did happen to fall ill in Venice, and then to "go off the rails" due to a sudden and potentially serious health issue. In short, there is a profound process of identification with the patient; or, one could say, an unconscious psychological process of understanding disguised by a banal association. However, on the most superficial level, Lori responds as an intellectual; yet, here too there is something else. She sets up Foucault in opposition to Proust: the homosexuality of the one is the link to that of the other and to her academic interest in the subject. Lori recalls her own past transgressions, which we can think of as a failed attempt to grab the bull by the horns, to expose herself to something that terrified her: the blood of the wound of sex, but also of the absence of the other. Everything suddenly precipitates towards the "homosexual" solution of the absence of difference, and towards the dramatic evocation of a kind of violence.

I start from the analogy of the missing cushion, from the fracture (?) at the base of the skull and the relative disconnection of the sensory floor of the ego, but above all from my own sense of vertigo, like someone who has lost the thread of a tangled skein; I take advantage of the unconscious psychological work done, and I try to say something that can help us make sense of things. Perhaps the analysis has to work for a long time, so to speak, in a "female homosexual" way. Ferro (2002, 2007) would represent it thus: (♀♀), as a relationship that in itself cannot be generative. The band of oscillation between the diverse points of view can only be very narrow, otherwise there would be "bloody" fractures in communication. It is true that without these there is no possibility of re-signifying old traumas. Everything lies in their sustainability. But Freud's warning that nothing can be destroyed in effigy remains valid. The school episode probably means that we must stop causing a disturbance: inadequate containment or capacity for reverie is experienced as active persecution.

I commented on the vignette using the principle of the absolute anti-realism of the analytic field (which obviously corresponds to the absolute realism of unconscious psychic reality!), of the here-and-now, but still following a principle that I would call *weak subjectivity*, halfway between a unipersonal psychology (a psychology of the subject) and a radically intersubjective theory. A reading that privileges the latter would see all the events of the field in a more impersonal way. For a moment it would suspend all reference to separate subjects (which is impossible in practice, since they are always in dialectical tension with the emotional field they unconsciously generate) and would read the session as if it were a narrative made up of characters and events narrated by several authors who would no longer be identifiable in the finished, and totally fictional, product. After all, the players of a multi-player video game are normally unknown to each other. They know nothing about their faces or their stories. *They only know their avatars.* And this is more than enough to engage in exciting games and learn to play (i.e. symbolise) better.

Dreams

18th May 2020, Last Day of Lockdown

It is the night before the Monday when the first lockdown is lifted. *We're driving to Genoa. At a turn in the road an intensely green hilly landscape comes into view – more Tuscan than Ligurian, extensive, beautiful. But the road proper comes to an end. It continues down to the right, but now it is a wide dirt road. They are building a motorway or maybe they are completely redoing the asphalt. I notice that there is a deviation, but it takes the opposite*

direction and goes uphill rather than downhill. After a while, I
continue on foot. The incline gets steeper and steeper and I find
myself climbing up a vertical wall of ice. I am distressed. I try to
look up but I cannot. I am unable to continue and I ask S., who is
farther ahead if she can see the top. I wake up.

Freud says that the navel of the dream is never found and even
this dream could be read in many different (but not necessarily
arbitrary) ways. However, at first sight, it seems to me that the
references to current events are plain to see. The uncertainty of the
next day (the motorway with no tarmac). The lockdown will end,
but the virus will still be around, albeit invisible. Then, there is the
invisible dimension of death: the wall of ice, solitude, the risk of
getting sick during this period and not surviving. But also the
finitude of life can be seen positively, as Freud (1916) states in his
brilliant essay "On Transience", as that which lies at the heart of
the feeling of beauty: the sea and the hills, which take me back to
the part of Italy where I was born.

However, the key moment – and the one I would like to emphasize – comes when I realize that I cannot see what is in front of me
(in actual fact, above me), and I ask for help. In the dream, I have
the intuition that this is the only way I can regain my humanity and
escape the no-man's-land of the nightmare. This point – whose
profound meaning is the appeal to the other, or the (re)discovery
that, we can only see (think; in Greek *theōrein* means "to see" and
"to consider" or "to speculate") thanks to the other that is in me
and sees for me and vice versa, etc. – could be discussed at length.

For example, we could ask ourselves: What do we talk about
when we talk about intersubjectivity? What becomes of Freud's
concept of the unconscious when seen in the light of intersubjectivity? What can we say about the discontent of the "civilization" in which we live? Are we condemned to unhappiness? Is it
true, as some say, that humanity as a whole (albeit with many
invaluable exceptions, of course) seems to be in the grip of an
irresistible drive towards self-degradation? And if mutual
recognition is not given within a relationship where there is
domination, what can each of us do, starting from our own
sphere, to create "devices" that can really bring about events of
authentic intersubjective recognition and, by doing so, counter-
act "degradation?"

The Lion King

A tormented night during which I wake up several times. I'm distressed by the alarming news of the coronavirus outbreak. *I dream I am in the garden of the house where I was born. On the other side of the fence, I can see the outline of an adult lion. I get scared and run to tell everyone that they should immediately lock themselves in the house. In another scene, which I don't know whether to place before or after, I see a little lion cub playing and running around in the garden with a dog or a house cat.*

When I am awake, I interpret the dream as a representation of a danger that I could not have anticipated or from which I have barely managed to escape. The next day, over lunch, I recount the dream to my family. My intention is to lighten up a little the general mood of concern. But actually, my reason for doing this is because it's a nightmare. It is like an attack of mental indigestion. The actors in my inner world, who are constantly conversing with each other as they stage – and thus lend meaning to – my emotional "dramas", can't cope on their own and decide to get help from an outside group. As one of the members of my family immediately points out: "It's obvious, the lion wears the crown ('corona,' in Italian)!"

The context of the dream is the one we are all living through (at the time of writing, nobody knows how it will end). On account of my age and because I cannot afford to stop working indefinitely, I feel I am the person most exposed to the risks of contagion, but also the one that could open the lion's cage. As head of the family, I am the "lion king" of the situation. The association with the Disney film makes me aware of the Oedipal implications of the whole situation. The day before I raised my voice with one of my children (in fact, the "cub" of the family) who, in my opinion, had not fully appreciated the danger and wanted to go out for an aperitif in the main square with his friends.

I also remember a similar dream I had at the beginning of my analysis, 30 years earlier, and that the word "lion" was contained in the name of my analyst, who died prematurely when he was about my age.

I also reflect on the fact that during this period, even before the official restrictions were introduced, I banned myself from visiting my very old parents, still living in the house that appeared in the dream. I would never want to be the bearer of the virus, the "crown", and so on. For someone familiar with certain themes, it is another way of realizing that the "crown" is never disjunct from the ghost of patricide (Oedipus, Karamazov, Macbeth and, of course, Hamlet: "The serpent that did sting thy father's life now wears his crown").

In telling this dream, I emphasize the function – which in *Beyond the Pleasure Principle* Freud attributes to dreamwork, and which Bion (1992) later expands to the full – of transforming fear (*Schreck*) into anguish (*Angst*). The former feeling is potentially traumatic, while the latter acts as a danger signal and thus preserves the ego. What I also emphasize is the fascinating and inextricable interweaving of motifs and generations, past and present, reality and unconscious fantasies, that make up the fabric of reverie and dreams.

Claustrophobia

A patient, Z, recounts a dream: "*I was in a house, I was very sick, I was very tired, I had some illness but the house was not dark, it was full of children playing, I had dark circles under my eyes. I went out into the garden and there were some quiet people, the sun was shining and in the middle of the garden there was a coffin, that coffin was for me and I was asking to be given something and put to sleep because going directly into the coffin was frightening me, I risked suffocating and getting sick … mamma mia… !*"

If this is no longer just the dream the patient had at night at home, but the dream *they* are having *together now* in the session in the act of telling it to each other, the meaning changes completely. It is no longer just the patient's nightmare of having a dead mother inside him, or of feeling suffocated inside a coffin-womb, of having, in short, a claustrophobic place in the mind. Hypothetically it would be the analytic relationship that has also become such. Why? We don't know, but the important thing is to ask the question.

It could be, for example, because the analyst tends to be a bit pedantic, to catechize the patient. For someone who already suffers from an excessive sense of duty, these implicit exhortations to change only plunge him deeper into crisis. The relationship becomes – and the word is precisely right – "suffocating". Analysis becomes a claustrum. The field signal delivered through the dream is powerful. It summons up a situation that is almost unthinkable from an emotional point of view. Even just thinking about it is distressing: like seeing Uma Thurman buried alive in *Kill Bill*, or the protagonist in *Burial*, or the scene in Buñuel's *Un Chien Andalou* where a man takes a razor blade and slices the eye of a woman looking straight at the spectator.

Transformation in dreaming

The vet analyst

A. starts the session by saying that her cat is unwell and that she has had to take it to the vet. Then she asks why she cannot hear the analyst's dog any more; is it perhaps not very well? Finally, she says that she has given up the idea of studying psychology and is thinking instead of veterinary medicine. She makes the point that with animals everything is "physiological" and there is no problem about having to interpret things. For this reason, she adds, she thinks she would be a very good vet; there would be no danger of failing.

Her reasoning clearly implies that there is too much anxiety in the air produced by the wish to understand things from the point of view of the theories of psychoanalysis and perhaps insufficient capability to empathize with the more "animal" aspects of the relationship. The analyst does indeed feed the patient, but on a vegetarian or sometimes even vegan diet, always paying attention to what to eat and what not to eat. All analysts should also study veterinary medicine, but "Everyone wants to be a psychologist", A. says, "no one wants to be a vet".

Lost in revision

I have to do a webinar supervision. The thing that immediately strikes me is that I received two versions of the patient's history in quick succession. The reason for this is simple. The analyst had continued to edit the text, removing some elements that might violate the patient's confidentiality and reveal his identity. However, if we consider this fact, only apparently external to the analytic field that is created not only in the analysis but also in the supervision, we can already consider it as part of the dream, or *nightmare*, in which the couple is trapped and from which they are asking to escape. "Dreaming", of course, for us means trying to make sense and give meaning to the emotional experience we share. Furthermore, the assumption is that the dream of the supervision session is in resonance with the dream of the analytic session and that it can therefore represent an expansion, evolution or transformation of it; that is, it can help make a shift from the climate of persecution experienced when a given thing is not understood to a climate of relief when this happens.

It is not important, nor would it be possible, to analyse how the two texts differ. We do know right away, however, that one version has been *withdrawn* and another has been made *public*. The opportunity here is to see this as a kind of action reverie, that is, as something that has been dramatized by the couple that we are at this point and that can potentially be used to intuit what is going on.

As I said above, it is important to resist the temptation of wanting to fill it too soon with a determinate meaning. For "didactic" reasons and for the sake of expositive clarity, however, here I will do the opposite. A small example of how the little "box" of preconception can be saturated by a fact which henceforth becomes illuminating might be when we read a sentence in the text that refers to the previous analyst: "the other one disclosed too much about herself". If we listen to this from the point of view of the shared dream of the session, this detail can prompt the question about how and whether something like this could be part of the way *this* patient and analyst interact. If the revised version of the text shows a greater concern about respect of confidentiality, then it follows by analogy that the action reverie of sending it can be seen as the analyst's dream (or rather the dream dreamt by the group of which she, along with me, is currently a part) about the possibility that some kind of 'lack of respect' in the session with the patient might be a problem in the analysis.

On a banal level, there could be a failure to take sufficient account of the principle of tolerability of interpretation, which might in turn lead unintentionally to a certain quantum of violence that is ultimately mutual. On this view, the patient feels exposed to an excess of "difference" and reacts, as we read in the text, with "nausea and murderous rage"; the analyst, in turn, is subjected to the insult of this aggression on the part of the patient.

Dementia

Patient S. is afraid he has Alzheimer's disease. The analyst reassures him. She has previously noted that she often feels pressured by this patient to be "a reasonable person". We know the very relative value of reassurance in analysis; yet, here a certain violence might lie in the fact that from another point of view, if we consider what the character "dementia" may mean in terms of unconscious communication and the analytic field, the "disease" could be that they both tend to be too "reasonable".

The field character of "dementia" might point to a certain inadequacy in the interpretation of its unconscious meaning. To treat the disease, the analyst should use a congruous degree of disciplined *unreason* or "dementia" in the form of negative capability and faith, i.e., listening without memory, desire and understanding.

The central point always revolves around the need to read the dialogue of the session as a theatrical text written jointly by two authors; this means that, from the point of view of unconscious interaction, it is impossible to tell who is responsible for any given line or page as opposed to another. This way of seeing, which truly implies a dramatic reversal of perspective, has important consequences.

For example, if we listen to a patient's complaints about a certain figure in his life as an allegorical narrative in which the couple or two-person group comprising analyst and patient tell each other about the quality of the air they are breathing, we can no longer explain things in terms of transference in the strict sense, nor can we give transference interpretations. The story that is being told in real time is no longer to be looked at with suspicion. The *we* replaces the *I/you*, and the *here and now* replaces the *there and then*. Again: to replace the *we* and the *there-and-then* does not mean cancelling them out; no more than when we shift from one view to another when looking at a bi-stable figure.

Psychic growth is achieved not when the subject absolutizes one vertex, but when he manages to multiply them and pass from one to the other. In this way he expands his possibilities. Emotion is precisely the reaction of the body that signals the movement whereby the subject brings about a significant change of vertex.

In this case, the analyst might think that the text the patient takes the trouble to read (but it could also be an analyst's own reverie) is the story they have written unconsciously together, and is therefore *true*, indeed *must be true*; also that it reflects an emotional climate between them that is marked by embarrassment, frustration, resentment, etc. Although the therapist is not the sole author of the text of the session, her role would dictate that it was up to her to change the atmosphere in the room. From this point of view, before the analyst has even pronounced a word, the main therapeutic factor lies in her ability to reclaim ownership of an emotion that was unconscious either because it was not recognized at all *or because it was attributed only to the patient* (*or only to the analyst*).

MOM

An analyst suggests that a patient should reflect on the link between her traumatic history with her mother and the way she reacts to breaks in the analysis, and also on the similarities between the analyst and her "MOM". This is a sensible and correct way to interpret. However, we could also try adding another lens (the technique ophthalmologists use when they measure a patient's myopia) to see if we can get a slightly clearer view.

One possible viewpoint could be to see "MOM" as one of the dance figures drawn by the analyst–patient pair. Such a figure (character, field hologram) would express their emotional truth at a given time or stage of analysis. As it is "shared" and does not belong to one or the other, we would think of it as something *already dialectically negotiated on the unconscious level*, therefore something necessarily true at least for them, as it is *their* point of view, and not immediately (or exclusively) traceable to a traumatic event in the patient's history. A memory of the past is nothing other than a way of digesting beta elements in the present.

By choosing to look at things from this angle, the analyst would wonder what she could do or say to change the air poisoned by a

MOM FUNCTION, a function that makes it impossible to communicate and that replaces true emotional attunement with a superficial mode of reassuring each other and merely exchanging "information". Significantly, on this view any talk about interruptions between sessions would be listened to as virtually referring to as interruptions of *in-session* contact.

Heaven and hell

T. describes the frustration he feels after having decided to isolate himself at home in a kind of voluntary quarantine, and associates it with a childhood memory. He hated going to kindergarten. From a little window in the nursery he used to look up at his nearby house, aching with "homesickness". "It was like heaven and hell", he tells me. This lasted until he started throwing up every time he had to go out and his mother stopped forcing him to do so.

Here, T. expresses his depressive experience in the situation of the pandemic, which means that he has to give up many vital opportunities for meeting people – at work, in his spare time and in emotional relationships. At the same time, he is probably alluding to the distance in our relationship, since the session takes place via the internet.

But there is also another possible perspective to take into consideration. "Hell" and "heaven" could be the images he uses (or rather "we use") to say when we are in contact and when we are not in the session, regardless of whether the session is remote or in person. The spatial description he provides is significant. At the top is the house-as-paradise and at the bottom the kindergarten-as-inferno. But isn't hell the spiritual condition in which everyone finds themselves when they feel *looked down* on from above?

The associations with the pandemic and the risks it entails for physical life is a way of symbolizing the intensity of the danger experienced in those separations, and also all the others. Each time separating from the object (from the other) is as if he were risking fatal pneumonia.

En passant, we note here the richness that the creative ambiguity of the metaphorical or allegorical expression ("*as if*") possesses compared to the merely conceptual or abstract expression. There is a clear gain in terms of sense (vividness, sensoriality, presence) and meaning (the multiplication of points of view). In order to appreciate the cognitive value of the "hallucinatory" image of a nocturnal dream (or hallucinosis, reverie, metaphor) and the true depth of raw emotions they struggle to contain, the "secret" is to fictionalize reality (the risk of bilateral pneumonia = fear of separation) and then to reverse the process and, as it were, concretize the "dream" (separation = true physical pneumonia).

In this way we rediscover the weight of psychic reality because we are very mindful of what the medical condition of bilateral pneumonia would entail. Moreover, I repeat: we should see it as the "bilateral pneumonia" that *truly* affects the field (patient *and* analyst), in other words, as the quality of the emotional function that links them. As in art, the fiction of figurative language grants us access to something that we feel is truer and more real than what mere perception gives us.

Going back to T., from a historical and intrapsychic angle, it is obvious that if it takes so little for him to feel "in sin", it is because he suffers from an insecure attachment. In other words, he has a strong fear of losing the love of the object on which he depends in order to exist. Consequently, he shows a tendency to interpret the norm rigidly. To differentiate himself from the object means in itself to "sin" and to embark on a journey to hell. Generally, once this equivalence is established, you begin to cohabit with a wolf. You enter the concrete and psychic sphere of a coarse life. If things go well, over time you learn to take on a "shepherd-dog function". It would be even better to develop a "Kevin Costner function" as in *Dances with Wolves* (Costner, 1990), or like "St. Francis" in the *Little Flowers of St. Francis* episode that takes place in Gubbio and during which he succeeds in speaking to wolves.

Again, adding another lens, through which I look at the growth of mind in the here and now, for me what matters is to see the patient's story, which undoubtedly has a value in itself; nothing prevents me from appreciating it as such, as what we are unconsciously living through in the session in terms of the vicissitudes of mutual recognition. The important thing is not just to think that the "wolves" are only in the past, or only in the patient's life, or only in his mind, but that they can also truthfully represent the atmosphere we are both experiencing in the here and now.

For example, after T. had finally listened to this childhood memory as a shared dream, I got a clearer sense of the chronic feeling of aridity I felt in the sessions with him, my tendency to be distracted, a certain annoyance at his continuous reiteration of the fact that he didn't know what to say and his requests for practical advice about a range of everyday problems. All these sensations perhaps corresponded to the difficulty we had at that time to occupy the dimension of playing and dreams, and therefore also to the "vomiting" of undigested elements.

It is up to the analyst (asymmetrically/consciously/as a separate subject), then, to interpret the shared dream or to bring the personal affection of each member of the dyad back to its shared matrix, so as to assume responsibility for them and, if necessary, to try to "change the weather". For example, if it has not rained for a long time, you need to do a rain dance. Let us not forget that the analyst's magic should consist in her ability to listen to the unconscious. The following brief vignettes, which involve transformations in hallucinosis (Civitarese, 2015b), will provide examples.

Slash

In the text prepared for the supervision, the analyst often indicates the patient and his relatives using a capital letter followed by a dot. A colleague in the group observes that she finds it difficult to empathize with the patient because the use of the single initial makes him or her too impersonal. Looking more closely, I notice that the letter is often followed by the specification of the family role – father, daughter, wife – *placed between two slashes*. For example: "B. and K. K./B.'s son/" or "B./wife/" or "F./son/". The result is a text in which caesuras, sudden cuts, or blades of light seemed to slice up all the characters in the story told by the analyst or limit their humanity.

Shortly before, there had been talk of skipped sessions and delays: it was as if the many "cuts" made by the patient (or, from a field perspective, by the analytic dyad) had to prevent excessively intense emotions from being brought out into the open during the session; but they were also a sign of an insufficient ability to transform raw sensoriality and emotions – perhaps because of the scars left by old traumas. Someone else had pointed out that, although the patient was disorganized, he was able to express difficult concepts with great depth and rare poetic talent. It occurs to me then that the slash (/) is also used to indicate the separation of lines in poetry.

These narratives bring to life simple letters and punctuation marks – as a very young patient of Melanie Klein's[2] does on a famous page. On the one hand, we deduce that the slashes or cuts of his wounds have given the patient the capacity to use the poetic caesuras with which he recounts his suffering; on the other, that the analytic couple seems to be working more on a semiotic than semantic level. There seems to be a relative disjunct between, on the one hand, the authenticity they both show and their ability to enter into a deep relationship, and, on the other, the possibility of using psychoanalytic concepts more precisely to register the first traces of turbulence in the analytic field.

For example, when reading the text, the analyst twice mispronounces *reveals* as *relieves*. Then, a couple of pages later, the patient tells her about a girl who committed suicide and observes that maybe her relatives felt *relieved*, because she drove them crazy. However, the analyst does not grasp the connection between these two points. Otherwise she might have considered her two "mistakes" as transformations in hallucinosis and read them in the light of the patient's comments on the girl. In this way, maybe she would have intuited that the patient was addressing a key question to her. Was she able to deal with his insanity, or would she instead feel relief at his "suicide", either in a concrete sense or, metaphorically, as a withdrawal from the relationship or breaking off of the therapy? As a matter of fact, the patient had been rejected by a previous therapist who had realized he could not help him.

Postpartum depression

A period of separation from the analysis is about to begin because my patient, P., is soon going to give birth. She says: "I'll see you after Easter... If, then, I happen to come down with severe postpartum depression..." For a moment, however, I understand: "If *you* happen to come down...". It's as if a transformation in hallucinosis had helped the "ordinary" unconscious to express the profound meaning – for her but also for both of us – of the emotional experience associated with the prospect of our impending separation.

Obviously, the homonymy in Italian between "parto" (childbirth), from the verb "partorire" (to deliver or to give birth) and "parto" ("I'm going to leave", from the verb "partire", to leave) plays a role here.

Woody Allen or Actor's Studio?

In comedy the twofold principle of redemption applies: in form and in content. When the comic register appears in analysis, it always represents something invaluable. For example, A. describes meeting a woman he was in love with by chance in a bar one evening. Because he was in the company of another woman, he decided to follow her into the bathroom to talk to her. Here, he explains, he felt like he was in a Woody Allen film. *For six minutes he held his hands under freezing water waiting for her to come out.* There was no hot water in the bathroom and he hates the cold. The analyst jokes about why he held his hands under a jet of icy water, suggesting that perhaps otherwise he would feel he was not being authentic. They laugh together at the scene. She says: "More than Woody Allen... it was an *Actor's Studio* thing... you know... where *it has to look real....*". A. replies that he was very excited, that they'll see what happens next, "and perhaps there might be another episode of *Beautiful* on this couch".

The couple's ability to play together is evident. The fact that they associate the story they are telling each other with a film by Woody Allen or with the TV series *Beautiful* only underlines the ability to symbolize what they have acquired together. Patient and analyst slip with great ease in and out of the worlds of reality and fiction. However, the six minutes of freezing, which we imagine as interminable, and the appearance at a certain point of the little word "hates" intimate that this (waiting for the object in a state of "primitive agony") is not only something that has possibly happened many times in the past, or that only reflects a type of relationality between internal objects, but that it is also what *is* happening or maybe *has just* happened in the session.

The purpose of interpretation, therefore, is always to take something that is far away and make it suitable for observation, that is, to bring it as close as possible. Just like in a famous Italian song by Gino Paoli ("Il cielo in una stanza" [The Sky in a Room]), each time the analyst takes "the sky" (something that is apparently very distant) and transports it into the consulting room. The change in perspective is immediate and surprising. Anything that is close to us is more suitable for observation and matters more to us. The beloved woman becomes the analyst for the patient and also, symmetrically, the patient for the analyst, but not as an object of transference. If anything, the transference already becomes a truthful and perceptive reading of the real qualities of the object.

Once again we realize how difficult it is to abandon a language that describes *who does what to whom* within a relationship between two separate objects. Strictly speaking, however, if we really take the fragment of analytic conversation as the continuous dream of the field constituted by the couple, then the "characters" we can dub "surprise", "anxiety", "frost" and "hate" would all be seen as emotional functions of the field; as a succession of rapid variations in climate, and whose new course the analyst must consciously try to influence in a positive sense. I repeat: an emotion may be "unconscious" in at least two different ways: first, because sometimes the emotion that is active at a given moment must be inferred from the story; second, because, although already evident in itself, it must be traced back not only to the analyst or to the patient, but to both. In essence, *even when it is an already conscious emotion, it is still unconscious if it is not read as the O of the session or as the "common" unconscious emotion in the here and now.* Not making this transposition would imply that the analyst is not yet taking responsibility for it.

In this vignette the analyst is relatively successful in putting a positive spin on things, that is, moving them in the direction of *at-one-ment* and recognition. By means of an unsaturated intervention – that is to say, one that seems everyday, banal or simply allusive and playful – she manages to share a liberating moment of humour (the human expression that is most steeped in true *pietas*) with the patient. In the dream-history of the session this state of mind stems from the mixture of embarrassment, acute desire and shame triggered by the unexpected moment of recognition at the "bar" that is the analytic room. How do we know in retrospect what the new bonding or climatic transformation is? We pay attention to the new characters that come onto the scene. In this case, the soap opera *Beautiful* appears: at the same time the signalling of a feeling of beauty but also the evocation of the tormented and tangled plots of this memorable and highly successful TV series. Moreover, it is the patient himself who unconsciously alludes to the transposition of the episode to the scene of the analysis when he mentions the analyst's couch.

Finally, it is difficult not to appreciate the metacommunicative value that the analyst's words have with regard to the theory of therapeutic action in analysis when he comments "... *it has to look real....*". Only what feels true and real can have any hope of bringing about changes in people's profound emotional world.

Doing somersaults

At the beginning of a session a patient describes how her personal trainer is teaching her how to do somersaults. She only needs to overcome one last obstacle and then she will have cracked it. This fills her with happiness. At first, she was afraid of getting hurt and was too tense, but now she realises that her body is learning. *It works.*

One possible way of listening to this story is to think of it as the couple's unconscious indicating to themselves that they are doing well when they can "play", that is to say, when they are on a level where the verbal explication of the meaning of what is happening in analysis does not override the non-verbal conversation – and therefore the development of functions and competences that are deposited in the body as affective concepts or implicit patterns of behaviour.

24/7

S. asks to cut down her number of sessions from three to two – so, one hour less per week. She often talks about a co-worker who is several years older than her and whom she depends on a lot. She likes to work with the co-worker, but can take her "only in small doses... not 24/7! She gets under my skin, she shows no respect for boundaries, I am going to try to get some space". For her part, even the analyst, despite her heavy investment in S., feels tense and finds the moments of silence challenging. The emotional atmosphere of the session seems to be impregnated with mutual expectations that are too pressing. It occurs to me that, instead of the urge to understand, it would help them if they could imagine that they were at a bar with a friend, just talking, and that they have all the time in the world to kill.

Let us now try to listen as analysts. The question would then be: What is the possible unconscious meaning of what S. is telling me about her colleague?

Interpreting within a field frame, we could transform S.'s comment into a dream: "We have dreamt of a rather annoying colleague and we need to find a little more space." We would no longer be seeing "the colleague" only as a real figure in the patient's external world, or as a possible vehicle for transference projection. Instead, we would also see her as the allegory of a totally *reciprocal* emotional function that is active in the field in the here and now.

Once the discourse, which apparently only deals with reality, has been listened to as a possible unconscious communication that the couple sends to itself, this does not mean that we automatically know what the prevailing emotion is, the O of the session.

For example, the "24/7" character might suggest that it is as if they never separate and that this is tiring. If I had to call it, I would say this seems the most likely meaning. They are telling each other that they spend too much time under each other's skin. As a consequence, the analyst would realize that: a) it is not the patient who unilaterally attacks the analysis by asking for a reduction of the sessions, but the reduction seems to be a request that arises from a common need; b) that there *really is* a "too much", something that is suffocating the analysis and is waiting to be decreased (fewer "doses"); c) that "the pressure" would not been reduced by a third, as the change from three to two sessions would seem to suggest, but only by a 24th, since what has happened is that 24/7 has become 23/7. Paradoxically, the 24/7 character might also suggest that, if they found the right fit, they would really have the pleasure of being together - hyperbolically expressed - all the time!

Abjection

The patient continually disparages the analyst, provokes her, even calls her an abject human being. By doing so, however, he makes himself obnoxious and almost physically disgusting. He distracts himself, he does not listen, and sometimes he is openly offensive, and so on. The analyst does not always manage to steer clear of this provocation, and they often end up engaging in something that looks a lot like bickering. The analyst, then, tends to give explanations and to stick to a fairly intellectual level. This situation lasts for very long periods of time.

Gradually, "in search of existence" (and survival), the analyst manages to avoid confrontations. She learns to tolerate silence better. She tries not to listen in terms of *I/you* but of we. She comes to understand "disgust" no longer as her feeling towards the patient or the patient's towards her but as a quality of the analytic field ("we dreamt that we kept finding each other repugnant"). In this way it becomes possible for her to think of disgust as abjection, that is, what Julia Kristeva (1980) sees as the child's need to separate itself from the mother's body. She is reminded of all the times when, seemingly inexplicably, the patient had told her that with her he felt as if he was being suffocated or swallowed up. She also intuits that this is the level – emotional, non-verbal – at which the most important game of analysis is being played. She has to allow this game of mutually triggered abjection to perform its function of establishing a more livable distance between them.

Lockdown or look down?

A: When you don't see me, in the times between sessions, you get angry.

P: The days are going to be long... what if there's a look down?

In the text drafted by the colleague for supervision there is a "slip of the pen": the analyst wrote *look down* instead of *lockdown*. But from our point of view we could interpret the "error" as a hallucinosis, i.e., a dream from which one wakes up (the event that actually makes a dream a real dream) and that therefore lends itself to being interpreted according to the concept/tool of transformation in hallucinosis. The interpretation would run as follows: the fear we have is not so much the coming separation, which is inevitable, but the fact that *now* I just felt (separated from you) because being on the receiving end of such a clever interpretation I felt treated with contempt and arrogance, as if *looked down* upon. It is obvious that the feeling would be entirely mutual. An analyst who were so reproached would in turn feel looked down upon by the patient.

The point then becomes to construe the "look down" quality as indicating a field-emotional function that needs to be changed. Indeed, feelings of humiliation and shame reflect the failure of the process of mutual recognition.

The pleasure of the hour of analysis

A patient says, "*I am in a building and I am hiding in a room, a woman opens the door and finds me. I have mixed feelings and am caught between the pleasure of being found and being discovered.*"

The obvious reading would be "between the *pleasure* of being found and the *fear* of being discovered". So when the analyst reads the text, she adds the word that had been omitted, namely "fear". However, we could ask ourselves the question: what does it mean, then, that she had (or rather, "they had") un-consciously omitted it, thus making us think the opposite, in other words, that it was "pleasure" in both cases? Possibly, beneath the apparent fear, the shared experience is in actual fact one of pleasure, of feeling recognized for what she really is and for what she is worth.

A Nutella diet

A., a patient, says that when she was a child, everyone in her house had to follow a very strict diet that left little room for chips, sausages, sweets, Nutella, hamburgers, spaghetti bolognese, ice cream. You had to be ultra-healthy. Every calorie was counted. In her teenage years she started to have problems with anorexia, and the problem never completely went away.

Obviously, A. is also describing the dietary regimen patient and analyst have prescribed for themselves in analysis, with everything designed to achieve high performance, which implies giving up the things that taste best. The analyst emphasizes the patient's self-hatred. However, in doing so she reminds her of her *madness*. She fails to consider that the whole question of "diets" might be about the veridical representation of how much truth-as-food-for-the-mind, according to Bion's definition of emotional attunement, they manage to provide for themselves and consume. In other words, both are suffering from a psychic diet that does not leave enough room for pleasure and play ("the things that taste best").

Reverie

What if I should meet her?

Throughout a whole session the analyst gives interpretations of the anger aroused in the patient, M., by the breaks between sessions and at the weekend, and often uses the metaphor of her infantile or "childish parts", etc. The patient, for her part, expresses feelings of irritation in various ways. She accepts the analyst's Kleinian flavoured interpretations but at the beginning of the session she speaks of the time when, as an adolescent, she used to eat too much, leaving her feeling ashamed and humiliated. She says that at home her ageing dog is about to die; it is constantly bleeding and may have to have its legs amputated. Then she recounts a dream in which the analyst appears undisguised and does not want to help her.

There is a lot of anger circulating in the room; M. speaks about it very openly. The impression, though, is that it is increasing rather than decreasing. The analyst gives interpretations in an orderly, coherent way, and in language that is simple and direct; still, she sounds formulaic, a bit mechanical, distant, bureaucratic. She says things like, "Maybe you haven't been so well, you are thinking about next weekend, you are afraid of being alone and that I might disappoint you. Not seeing me is like taking away your ability to walk, like cutting off your legs."

M. talks about a friend and the idea of founding an association to do something to help children in need, but the cue is not picked up as an invitation to truly attend to her bleeding aspects. The interpretation of M.'s frustration over breaks translates, instead, into calling attention to a reality principle that M. *should* accept.

In supervision, having finished reading the session, the colleague involved mentions a conference that will be taking place soon, where she might see her patient, and says, "What if I should meet her?" Here, the image of this scene, one that might actually come to pass, can be regarded as a *reverie*. The emotion it reflects has to do with embarrassment, shame, risk, judgement.

If we consider the reverie to be a shared dream, regardless of who the spokesperson is, we can see it as a channel of access to these unconscious feelings that are present not only in the patient but also in the analyst (the basic assumption or the O of the session). By listening in this way, the analyst would be relying on the representational capacity of the shared or "third" unconscious. She would not construe it, for example, as countertransference, which would ultimately reflect the distortion the patient is responsible for because of her transference. Instead, she would ask herself how to move on from the shame and perhaps avoidance that in some ways seem to characterize their relationship, and come to the point of actually meeting each other.

At any event, the decisive step lies in the change of perspective, in the mode of listening. "What if I should meet her there?" becomes not only the representation of a vital risk, fraught with a certain anxiety, or perhaps even anguish, but also a possibility, that is to say, the expression of a desire, the prefiguration of a more intimate and authentic way of being together and of "existing"[3] each other.

I repeat, the question should be listened to as a reverie, and not only as the anticipation of a concrete event that might occur in the near future. It would be: "we dreamt that we wondered: what if we were to meet?" It would be clear that the real meeting is one of recognition in the session, not at a seminar or conference held in a university lecture hall.

Incidentally, there are shadows but also light in this session, even if the light remains in the shadow cone of formulaic interpretations. For example, at a certain point in the report of the session, M. says that she feels her mother's concern, which she understands as rejection, when she tells her not to take the tram to the city centre alone but to go with her friend: "I take this badly and it is as if she were choosing my friend over me. I understand that it is a way of worrying about me, but that's not the way I experience it, I feel rejected." However, the analyst misreads the words said by the patient, and, instead of "as if she [*lei*] (which in Italian is also the courtesy form for "you") were choosing my friend over me", she reads, "as if *Lei* [which usually has the capital letter when used instead of 'you' to address someone formally] were choosing *me*", which is equivalent to saying, "as if YOU [*lei*] were choosing ME".

In other words, she makes the patient say that she does not feel rejected at all, and rather "chosen" or recognized by the analyst. If we see the slip as a transformation in hallucinosis, we could interpret it as a dream *à deux* from which you wake up when the mistake is realized. Its meaning could be: somehow, unconsciously, despite my/your (our) feeling of being rejected, at a deeper level of the relationship we *are* choosing each other; in other words, we are beginning to recognize one other (in essence, to feel linked by an emotional bond).

Notes

1 Lateral transference consists in the manifestation of affects that express in a symptomatic way unconscious desires of infantile origin not directed at the analyst but at other figures or activities. In general, the phenomenon takes on the meaning of resistance.

2 See Melanie Klein (1924, p. 318):

For little Fritz in *writing* the lines mean roads and the letters ride on motor-bicycles – on the pen – upon them. For instance, "I" and "e" ride together on a motor-bicycle that is usually driven by the "I" and they love one another with a tenderness quite unknown in the real world. Because they always ride with one another they became so alike that there is hardly any difference between them, for the beginning and the end – he was talking of the small Latin alphabet – of "I" and "e" are the same, only in the middle the "I" has a little stroke and the "e" has a little hole.

3 This verb should be used also in the active mood: I exist you, or you exist me.

Chapter 6

Current controversies

What happens to the subject?

There's no bad end to it. The subjective side of what we call "subject", as we have already said, is strengthened every time we weave the threads (links, linkings) of intersubjectivity, if it is true that they are two sides of the same coin or like the warp and weft of a fabric. This is why it is important to build a convincing ontological and metapsychological model of the subject: to avoid the false dichotomy between subjectivity and intersubjectivity. The fact is that the more a person is "infinite", i.e., the more she is part of a growing human community, the more perspectives she has on things, and the more mature or free she becomes. Conversely, the more a person is part of a limited community, perhaps blindly obeying a small number of rigid principles, the poorer she is, lacking in true agency. The difference is like that between a democratic regime of the mind governed by ethical principles and a tyrannical regime governed by moralistic principles. Under favourable conditions, both individual and group find themselves in a win-win situation.

What happens to external reality?

External reality and past history are nonetheless the subject of endless conversations with the patient and are examined in all their different aspects. (What else should we talk about in

DOI: 10.4324/9781003219972-6

therapies that last for years and at a frequency of several sessions per week?) And yet nothing prevents the analyst, in her head, from adding a further and more sophisticated plane of understanding, without having to make any of it explicit to the patient. Psychoanalysis has this specific quality, namely, that it is based on the concept of the unconscious. Psychotherapy, in its strict definition, remains more on the concrete level of discourse and relies more on rational understanding.

The criticism is frequently made that Bion and BFT show a disregard for historical reality and trauma. Apart from the fact that this criticism seems to me completely off-target, it is nonetheless interesting if we consider it in terms of *its symptomatic value of identifying a clear difference from both distant and closely related theories*. To me, it's proof that BFT, like it or not, is more radically intersubjective than others, according to both the meanings we have given to that term, phenomenological and metapsychological. What does this mean? It means that as far as the symmetrical unconscious plane of the analytic field is concerned, it is more inclusive. It takes in more things. Otherwise it would be difficult to understand why criticism is aimed specifically at this quality of radical inclusiveness.

Obviously, it is not a question of denying the significance of past history, biography and even less so the importance of material reality; what matters, however, is rigorously taking into account the intersubjective vertex, taking for granted the obvious conscious vertex of the subject. The psychic reality of the couple and material reality are always to be kept in dialectical – as well as intrapsychic and interpsychic – relation to each other. Indeed, if we agree with Bion that what counts in analysis is what is true, we must privilege the present moment and keep in the background (but not obscure) the view of the other as a separate subject, or only acknowledge it later. We can play "the game of biography" with the patient, but even in this case the focus would be on the development of the capacity to play (the expansion of the psychic container), and less on the type of game itself. For Bion, and even more so for BFT, the term "comprehending" applies in the double sense of "taking in" and "understanding"; but then, just to complicate things, through the principle of negative capability/faith (Civitarese, 2019b), it also means forgoing abstract understanding.

In analysis, it is necessary to maintain this conjunction between reality and fantasy and between conscious and unconscious. In my opinion, some psychoanalytic models do not do this enough. They emphasize factual or material reality in two opposing and yet coinciding ways: either they tend to undervalue the discourse of the unconscious, as in certain forms of interpersonalism, or else they remain entangled in a non-rigorous conception of unconscious fantasy and communication between unconsciouses, while naively claiming to reconstruct the patient's actual history. To use Freud's image, it is as if reality interposed itself each time like a fire to interrupt the performance in the theatre of analysis. We should not forget that psychoanalysis is based on the paradigm of dreams as a way of reaching or, as we would say nowadays, of expanding the unconscious.

Sometimes a misunderstood concept of countertransference as a conscious and real-time perception of the analyst's experiences of the relationship is passed off as the transference reactivation of the patient's original neurosis or psychosis, sometimes right from the very first session. The analyst observes her patient through the prism of her ready-made countertransference. As we can see, the concept of the unconscious becomes evanescent. The analyst fails to hypothesize that, if it is a matter of countertransference, this lies in the automatic, hasty consultation of the theory about the sensations felt consciously more than in the sensations themselves, and that perhaps this is where the real game is being played. Why? *Because emotionally it is more difficult and sometimes painful; because it implies a closer engagement with the unconscious; because there is a higher price to be paid when tolerating doubt.* Instead, what we have is the omnipotent aspiration to construe transparently what happens moment by moment – of course, *every* psychoanalytic model runs this risk; yet, can we think that some models possess stronger antibodies against this virus?

Maybe this is the reason for Bion's caustic assertion that the only thing the analyst can do with her countertransference is to have it analysed by a colleague. As a matter of fact, few jargon expressions are so (annoyingly) ubiquitous and ritualistic in psychoanalytic literature as the pairing of transference and countertransference; and then, depending on the context, followed by: dynamic, pair, dyad, binomial, etc. A veritable litany which, one often suspects, is repeated even though its true meaning has been lost. The wear and tear on the concept is palpable.

But there is yet another litany: the rhetoric of trauma and testimony. The idea is that when faced with real trauma (who decides what falls into this category and what doesn't?) one must suspend analytic listening and only listen in a respectful and receptive manner – which, in fact, would always be the case. These analysts often demonstrate an astonishing deafness to the unconscious, and outside of what they believe to be the sacred area of trauma, they torment the patient with incessant guilt-inducing interpretations without even questioning the role that their own desire plays in the relationship.

The dream or unreal climate of the session

Expressions like dreaming the session or the shared/co-created dream can be easily misunderstood. Some think that they describe an excessively relaxed atmosphere in the session, a situation in which patient and analyst do nothing but exchange vague and ethereal fantasies. There would be much to say about such caricatured depictions. Here, it is sufficient to recall that for Bion the unconscious is a function of personality, that "dreaming" is synonymous with symbolizing (which can only happen intersubjectively), and that thus we dream even during the day.

Therefore, these are nothing more than formulas that highlight a style of work in which not only the subjectivity of the patient but also that of the analyst, as well as the unconscious functioning of the couple are taken seriously and as systematically as possible. In short, the dream and the unconscious lie at the centre of analysis: *Is there a project that is more Freudian in spirit than this?* What this angle of vision deconstructs are naively empathic attitudes or attitudes which involve an uncritical levelling down to the already known and to the presumed given of reality or concrete "fact".

To privilege the internal history of the relationship may give the impression that it amounts to neglecting the past of the patient's history, but in my opinion this is not the case at all. The past is and remains important. The point, however, is that for Bion and BFT *the present is even more so*. In what sense? In the sense that

Bion also sees the fact of re-signifying the past as an intimately intersubjective process of searching for truth; a truth, mind you, understood in the twofold significance of sense and meaning. What matters, then, is whether a shared truth is created also about this past or about the patient's factual reality. Therefore, in the analyst's receptive listening to the unconscious dimension of the patient's discourse, the truth of the emotional unison (*at-one-ment*) comes before the content related to the reconstruction of the past. If the analyst places value on the past in itself, regardless of any negotiation of mutual status as a person, as the social mask we all inevitably wear and which defines our identity, and of the dialectic of recognition that makes for analysis, she runs the risk of over-valuing the content irrespective of what is deemed "true" – or in other words, what is tolerable for both members of the analytic couple.

Is Bion a mystic?

To think of Bion's thought as a form of mysticism is truly a gross misunderstanding. Bion simply borrows new terms from other disciplines for his own purposes, which are scientific – of course, in a way that the humanities can be said to be "scientific". However, the adjective here should not be taken in a simplistic sense. Throughout his work Bion formulates a closely argued critique of the ideology of science. Bion's alleged mysticism is nothing other than a social (non-positivistic) theory of truth and a conception of healing as a radical and rigorous practice of receptivity to the productions of the unconscious of the analytic couple. It is like saying that interpretation is a little more at home in listening (when it is implicit) and less in what one says (when it is explicit) to the patient, and that such an approach is resolutely opposed to any form of *sentimentality* or *empathism*.

Bion says that by avoiding memories, desires and understanding, the analyst can approach the field of dreaming and hallucinosis, which are the most effective tools she can use to enter into unison with the "hallucinations" of her patients and, consequently, to learn from the experience. Such an attitude is proper to an analyst who has "faith" (another term imported from mysticism but which Bion adapts for technical use – basically a reformulation of the Freudian precept of evenly suspended or free-floating listening) in the possibility that the unconscious can be made to work.

So, concepts like *faith, O, nameless dread, becoming, evolution*, etc., are by no means religious concepts. They are useful because of the "penumbra" of associations they evoke (and not, as Bion points out, their bright light). The point of their introduction and use is (in opposition to logical/rational thinking) to promote the mental state conducive to developing the capacity for *intuition*. For example, the concept of negative capability and faith could be reformulated as excluding, at the pole of sensitivity, the intentional acts of perception and, at the pole of intellect, acts of understanding, in order to produce the maximum possible number of emotional pictograms and images. Because of their unsaturated, open and ambiguous nature, and because of the oscillatory (dialectical) functioning of the imagination or of dream thought, this is the "middle realm" where we see things from several points of view and therefore in a holistic, emotional and conceptual way. This is why they seem real to us, and ourselves with them.

Incidentally, intuition is just a term to be set in opposition to what philosophers call "sensible intuition" (i.e., perception), to mean a perception that is turned inward. Ultimately, by "intuition" we mean not something vague and elusive, but the analyst's ability to use the theories of psychoanalysis to access the dream spectrum in the session, and consequently the unconscious processes of the mind. If, following Bion, we call this access "intuition", it is to emphasize its complexity and highly conjectural nature – what is in fact a hyperbolic exercise of reversible perspective.

How does the analyst know that a reverie has to do with the patient and is not just rooted in countertransference?

This is also a frequent objection. The answer is very simple: *the question does not make sense.* Reverie and countertransference belong to different theoretical frameworks, they fit into different networks of concepts. Above all, *they arise from different postulates.* If my basic postulate is that any event or fact of analysis arises from the dynamic gestalt of the analytic field – a concept that is formulated to give a more satisfactory view of what happens on the unconscious plane of the relationship – then by definition nothing that appears as a phenomenon of analysis belongs only to one or only to the other. This is the case independently of the progressive or regressive quality reflected in it.

It is true, however, that long before the concepts of enactment, third and analytic field, those of countertransference and projective identification had already expressed, in some way, the central paradox of the dialectic of recognition, that is, the process of mutual alienation – the self becoming other and vice versa, thus establishing a shared area of the self – in which the process of becoming a subject lies.

Chapter 7

The new psychoanalytic critique

One of the many various faces of psychoanalysis is its theory of aesthetic experience. Let us think back to Freud's essays on Dostoevsky, Jensen, Leonardo, Hoffman, etc. Even today, psychoanalysis, especially the variant that takes inspiration from Lacan, is very present in the humanities departments of universities. Numerous authors make a creative use of it. The new psychoanalytic criticism is no longer the now rather discredited variant that put authors and characters on the couch and invariably found the same psychic complexes, doing so without paying the slightest attention to the essential aspect of the artistic product, namely its *form*.

The more traditional Freudian criticism is therefore unconvincing especially when it works from the same positivist assumptions that have become obsolete in the theory and technique of treatment.[1] We would be unable to appreciate the significance of this crisis if we did not relate it to a broader philosophical and cultural crisis. The so-called end of the "grand narratives" has made other critical approaches outside the Freudian sphere equally obsolete. However, we must remember that psychoanalysis itself gave a decisive impulse to the establishment of such a climate by undermining the foundations of classical philosophy and psychology's conception of the subject.

It is natural then that there have been attempts to use Bion's new theories and BFT to engage once again in a dialogue with art. Here I would just like to mention some of my contributions

DOI: 10.4324/9781003219972-7

on this topic and to give a brief outline of them. This is what I tried to do *in Losing your Head. Abjection, Aesthetic Conflict and Psychoanalytic Criticism* (Civitarese, 2018): namely, to inaugurate a style of engagement with art that is no longer one-directional, so to speak, but inspired by a principle of reciprocity. Psychoanalysis helps us to grasp the essence of the artistic experience, and art illuminates the processes whereby the aesthetic experience that is lived in the analytic session fosters the growth of the mind. Not only that; the exercise of interpretation does not aim to reduce the work to some invariable unconscious psychological constants that psychoanalysis is able to reveal. Rather, it seeks to highlight its creative ambiguity, to expand, in a sense, the artist's dream. In essence, the art work promises to help those who are exposed to it to develop functions as opposed to finding definitive truths.

The inspiration to write this text came to me from the many images of "sacred representations" in Italian museums, especially in Renaissance painting. The so-called sacred representation scene or Mother or Madonna with child seemed to me a perfect allegory of a good primary relationship with the object. Conversely, I took the figure of beheading, equally and surprisingly widespread, as an allegory of a failure of the same relationship. Beheading then served as a leitmotiv, which I examined in various artistic productions, from literature (Boccaccio, Thomas Mann, Corrado Govoni), to cinema (Michael Haneke, Ingmar Bergman, Joseph Losey, Shinya Tsukamoto), and finally to the video installation of the AES+F Group.

Another source of inspiration was the thinking of Jacques Derrida, who, as we know, owes much to psychoanalysis, and his practice of reading and unravelling texts that goes under the label of deconstruction. In the name of a receptiveness that we can define as "postmodern", I have tried to pay more attention to the rhetorical or formal aspects of the text and thus to avoid any interpretative closure. This does not mean that, however potentially infinite, we cannot continue a conversation about correct or unacceptable readings – not on the basis of some absolute principle but only in relation to the community within which such judgements are made. The challenge has therefore been to accept even in this field the possibility of continuous reversals of perspective in which art and aesthetic criticism, in a game of mutual mirroring, also illuminate aspects of the analytic process and highlight the rhetorical figures of its theory and its very character as fictional narrative or myth.

Such an operation has solid roots only with regard to the new conception, introduced by Bion, of the unconscious and dreaming, and the reference (which we owe to Ferro) to the writings of Umberto Eco, in particular to *The Open Work*, which deals with the role of the reader. In essence, it is no longer a matter of "applying" psychoanalysis to art, but rather of asking ourselves, with Pierre Bayard (1999), whether it is possible to do the opposite. In the book I interlaced my vision of psychoanalysis with that of Meltzer, using in particular the concept (which he took from Bion) of "aesthetic conflict",[2] and with that of Julia Kristeva, to whom we owe the concept of "abjection".

Put briefly, deconstructing the dream of the text no longer follows the police procedural logic of looking for the culprit, but rather the artistic logic of re-assembling discarded, secondary or marginal products in surprising new configurations. As in *bricolage* and in the corresponding artistic version of the ready-made, the key words are empiricism, contingency, ateleology, improvisation, play, opportunity, cunning, flexibility, movement, attunement, adaptability and amateurism (in the noble sense of cultivating an art not as a profession but with pleasure, passion, dedication and constancy).

Aesthetics of the sublime

I then explored the topic of psychic birth, that is, the plane of non-verbal, emotional-sensory communication in which a first glimmer of subjectivity begins to form, in *L'ora della nascita. Psicoanalisi del sublime e arte contemporanea* [The Hour of Birth: Psychoanalysis of the Sublime and Contemporary Art] (Civitarese, 2020b). (2020). The artists I deal with in this book are Richard Sierra, Anish Kapoor, Alexander McQueen, Anselm Kiefer, Nalini Malani, Sun Yuan, and Peng Yu. Their often monumental works are perfect examples of the contemporary sublime. Indeed, the point that the theory of the birth of the psyche must clarify is how it is possible for one mind to develop from another mind, when the nascent mind is still in a state of being without access to the semantic meaning of language. The psyche never stops being "born". In "normal" or pathological situations, it is always a matter of enlarging the space of the mind in which potentially destructive emotional content can be received and transformed.

As I scrolled through the list of original concepts that Bion forged in order to describe how psychic birth takes place, I was struck and intrigued by the numerous references he made to authors from the Romantic period of English literature and by a whole series of expressions drawn directly from that sphere. I then wondered whether the aesthetic concept of the sublime, in Bion's thinking, more or less subtly plays the role of a fundamental theoretical operator (Civitarese, 2014). For instance, Bion takes from Keats the concepts of "negative capability" and "language of achievement"; he quotes Milton and Coleridge; he talks about Faith, Madness, Genius, Infinity, the Mystic, Nothingness, Night, No-thing, Passion, Suffering, Infinity, Catastrophic Change, Mathematical Sublime, Nameless Terror, Astonishment, Tiger-The-Thing-Or, Thing-in-itself, and so on.

In my opinion, the concept of sublimation needs to be reinvented in a relational sense – no longer a kind of description of the psychic hydraulics of sexual drives but of the process of "social" construction of human subjectivity. If, then, we accept the idea that exploring these resonances or transpositions can tell us something new and interesting, and move us in various directions, then one possible gain we can take from direct contact with art is the understanding *from within*, emotionally, that it makes accessible (or more easily accessible) to us.

When we say that something is sublime, even in everyday life, we allude to a feeling rather than an understanding. It is a lived experience, for which we have no words, something that has to do with pleasure, beauty, feelings of vitality and personal integration. In fact, it cannot be put into words. Literally, it is ineffable (*not-sayable*). Yet, for us this experience is the pinnacle of what we can achieve. It is not only something that we can "experience" because we are, so to speak, already endowed with this sensitivity; rather, *we feel that the experience itself "gives" us this capacity, sharpens our senses, makes us grow psychically, "takes" us a little higher.*

In what direction?

In the direction of becoming ourselves. Who could say that they have really become themselves, that is, that they have fulfilled all their human possibilities? The paradox is that becoming oneself, being able to have a "greater soul", goes hand in hand with becoming infinite, if by this expression we mean the ability to have as many perspectives on things as possible. Under favourable conditions, this capacity arises out of conscious and unconscious intersubjective commerce with others.

We might think of the concept of ambiguity in poetry or dreams. Each time, poetry and dreams present us with precisely this extraordinary opportunity to have several points of view on the world (as many interpretations) but, insofar as they are explicitly and implicitly shared, they are not arbitrary. It is then that I can call myself a mature (or healthy) person, when I can escape from the system of mutilating splits (which I mentioned above) that limit my humanity, and, for example, force me, because I am in the grip of fear, to take a narrow, closed, fanatical or fundamentalist view of things.

As is readily clear, the problem in analysis is to promote growth (playing with metaphors, our PGI or psychic growth index) that does not take place in a split-off manner. With Winnicott,[3] we could say that it is always a matter of giving the body back to the psyche or of reinserting the psyche in the body – what Merleau-Ponty (1945b, pp. 86–87) would describe as "fusion of soul and body in the act, the sublimation of biological existence in personal existence and of the natural world in the cultural world".

But then we leave the paradigm of a psychoanalysis that thinks it is treating the patient because it translates the unconscious into the conscious. We think more of a psychoanalysis that makes automatic, habitual, acquired and unconscious the relational competence that at the beginning can only be absorbed passively. A logic of mere knowledge – in actual fact, it has never been only such, but it is true that even the experience of the analytic relationship (the so-called transference neurosis) in the end has always been put at the service of the reconstruction of the patient's real past – gives way, as Freud (1930, p. 130) says at the end of *Civilization and Its Discontents*, to the logic of *Liebe*, of love, of linking ("the experience of being loved [*Liebeserfahrung*]").

As we can see, for psychoanalysis, rethinking theory also in the light of the aesthetics of the sublime, and therefore having a clearer idea of what it means to speak of the social and aesthetic constitution (in the sense of being based on sensations) of the subject, implies renewing its conceptions of the unconscious, of dreaming and of thinking, and its technique. As one of the most advanced currents of contemporary psychoanalysis, BFT arises out of the encounter with the model of child psychoanalysis inaugurated by Melanie Klein based on the equation play = dream and the understanding Bion attained about the psychology of groups. In my opinion, the opportunity we now have with regard to the future development of the discipline is to abandon psychoanalysis as a school of suspicion (Ricoeur, 1965). In order to do this, we need to go beyond a way of listening to the unconscious based on an I/you split, on who does what to whom consciously and unconsciously. What matters most to me is instead being able to intuit the third or radically intersubjective dimension in which we see the "we" at work in the unconscious construction of meaning. I assume that the unconscious "we" is always at work in determining the so-called facts of analysis. This allows me to recognize in the "we" also the other as separate, and I am less likely to slip into ideological attitudes.

The heart of the analytic process becomes, as we see clearly depicted in allegorical terms in the classical paintings of the Romantic period (for example, by Turner, David Friedrich, etc.), the "right distance". The right distance is that which makes for a successful dialectic of identity and difference. In art, the measure of this "happiness" lies precisely in the pleasure we take from it. But this pleasure is always *negative*; it always has to do with the personal enrichment that comes from the intrinsically social possibility of "dreaming" anguish and transforming it. It is from this transformation that, for example, as Freud (1920) says in *Beyond the Pleasure Principle*, we paradoxically take "high enjoyment" even when we witness tragedy in the theatre. Firstly, what we witness is never just the misfortune of Antigone or Oedipus, but our own; secondly, it is no longer a tragedy at all but what we might call the miracle of form – *a consensuality that is lived, implicit, procedural, affective and semiotic more than merely thought.*

It would be wrong to see something masochistic in little Ernst's *fort-da* game, so wonderfully described by his grandfather Freud. Instead, this is the intense, exciting pleasure of existing (Winnicott: *going-on-being*). It is achieved by gradually elevating oneself above animality, by learning to use symbols. As the philosophers explain, *ek-sistere* means to come out of oneself, or rather, to engage in the paradoxical game of being both oneself and other than oneself.

The prototypical situation of the aesthetics of the sublime envisages a spectator witnessing a human or natural spectacle whose content and dimensions both frighten and attract. Seas of ice, storms, erupting volcanoes, monumental ruins, deserts, gorges, mountain peaks – but also shipwrecks or, as in the example given by Longinus in his treatise on the sublime, the terrible silence of Ajax in Hades. The question is: how is it that something that should make us want to run away ends up enchanting us?

Kant's explanation, namely the ability of human reason to go with the mind beyond the limits that nature imposes, does not convince me at all because it is too abstract. What fascinates is not horror *per se* but the horror that is redeemed by the body's capacity for thinking; not by abstract rationality, but by *form* – the aesthetic pleasure one experiences when one comes into contact with beauty. Of course, from the point of view of psychology, we cannot be satisfied with understanding form only as the perfection of colours, lines, sounds, volumes, etc. We must get an idea of why this is the case. We must get an idea of why beauty is necessary to life; or why, as Keats says, it is "truth". My take on this is that the form that we call beautiful or sublime or even "true", and which at birth is the *dynamic sensorial space* that structures the newborn as a subject, through a process of intersubjective mirroring/recognition, attracts the child as in itself it contains a promise of existence. *Indeed, it is the indispensable precondition for psychic birth*. We understand better why Proust (1992, p. 335) speaks of Baudelaire and his search for "reminiscences" or for "transposed sensation[s]": "in the perfume of a woman, for instance, of her hair and her breast, the analogies that will inspire him and evoke for him 'the azure of the sky immense and round' and 'a harbour full of masts and pennants'". It is easy to recognize in this extraordinarily evocative quotation some of the stylistic features of the aesthetics of the sublime.

So what truth are we talking about?

I think we are talking about something that also has to do with recognition, at-one-ment, being in unison, with a kind of "happy conversation" with the other that coincides with the process of subjectivation or becoming a person. In fact, if we go back to where we started, that is, to Bion, one of his guiding ideas is precisely that truth – not in a metaphysical, positivistic or absolute sense – is emotional unison; or rather, emotional unison is the truth that nourishes the mind. It seems to me a very timely concept of truth as inherently pragmatic and social. Not only that; it is also a concept of truth that is not split-off, not intellectualistic, but which instead contemplates what Heidegger would call our emotional *openness* to the world. In fact, there is no truth that is not also based on an emotional tonality.

When it comes to clinical work, anyone who seeks treatment has suffered from one of two opposite and coinciding forms of absence of the object. Either they have been abandoned, materially or figuratively, that is, emotionally (they have not been invested), or they have been invaded or intruded upon by the object. These are two different forms of "absence", but they coincide in their ability to generate a climate of fear and persecution that does not facilitate personal development and integration. Let us say, then, that the analyst is a bit like the painter who has to make terror thinkable and transform it into an aesthetic experience – the latter to be understood not as something superficial, in the sense of "aestheticizing", but rather as the quintessence of what makes us human.

Aesthetic experience as a sensory dimension of symbolization

Psychoanalysis is a hermeneutic discipline and (fortunately) not a science in the manner of the sciences of matter, and it has speculative thought as its privileged interlocutor. At the same time, because of the originality of the Freudian *Junktim* [4] – that is, the conjunction of theory and practice – it can aspire to say something about the essence of humanity that no other discipline can say in the same way.

If it seems reasonable to us to assume that the aesthetic theory of the sublime is an indirect way of theorizing how the psyche comes into being, and if it seems reasonable to see in the art inspired by the sublime an allegorical way of advancing this theorization, whose particular "metanarrative" quality we recognize – I mean that it does not belong exclusively to it, since, after all, any form of art can only embody the same principles, even that which appears as "simply" beautiful or pleasant – then it follows that what we are dealing with is *the very origin of symbolization.*

From a psychoanalytic point of view, the first element of symbolization can be seen in the "punctiform" tactile sensation generated by "happy" contact, that is, the contact that generates "order", between the baby's mouth and the nipple, or between the cheek and the breast (Ogden, 1989). When things go well, a form is born there that "contains"[5] anguish, and that becomes the prototype of other ever more complex "forms", which will be deposited in structures of the psyche. One understands that, from the outset, the psyche is intersubjective and that the tactile "coordination" described above between mother and child is merely the prototype of any subsequent mode of mutual recognition, even the most sophisticated one based on linguistic and conceptual skills. This is why it is important to see the child not as an isolated entity but as immediately constituting a system or field. If we fragment this group of two into its original elements, it is no longer clear how specific properties can gradually emerge.

Now, what happens when this happy "sensory" conversation is created – but still immersed in a symbolic context, since, although the child is "infans", the mother on the other hand, at least indirectly, brings culture and sociality into the relationship? Obviously, this cannot last. Immediately the feeling vanishes. Only the memory remains. The memory, at this point obviously on a procedural or implicit level, is the punctiform sensation that begins to transform itself into *something that stands for something else* – and which will then become the point, the line, the letter of the alphabet (Civitarese and Berrini, 2022), etc. Symbolization arises from a double absence: from the negativization of pain into pleasure, and from the negativization of this experience, positive in itself, into a mnestic trace. Absence, however, must be *tolerable.*

What makes absence tolerable? The fact that it does not *last* too long. If it lasts too long, the "no-breast", that is, the tolerable absence, or even the internal (and, in this sense, symbolic) presence represented by the mnestic trace of the experience of gratification starts to become anguish and then "nameless terror". At which point, the way to psychosis is open.

We should therefore conventionally differentiate the *no-thing* or *no-breast*, out of which thought arises, from *noughtness* as the total erasure of the trace, and thus also of the capacity to represent. The negative (the terrible, the dreadful), in short, dwells in the innermost fabric of our being. What we experience as self-awareness and a sense of personal autonomy and a centre of initiative is merely the developed and printed photograph of the negative that is its necessary prerequisite. We all always run the risk of sinking from *no-thing* into *nothingness* – of course, it is not an all-or-nothing affair. Referring once again to painting, it would be like falling into a glacier (as in David Friedrichs's *The Sea of Ice*), drowning in the sea like Leander (as in Turner's *The Parting of Hero and Leander*), etc., or having no idea of the existence of landscapes that awaken our sense of wonder and, as someone once put it, allow us to "be born", to "exist".

Further readings

Before closing this chapter, I would like to mention two books that in my view boldly and skillfully use Bion's theories and FT to explore the field of art. The first, by Kelly Fuery (2018), is entitled *Wilfred Bion, Thinking, and Emotional Experience with Moving Images: Being Embedded*. The second, by Robert Snell (2020), is entitled *Cézanne and the Post-Bionian Field: An Exploration and a Meditation*. Another work which refers extensively to Bion but that, despite evincing important convergences with it, is not an expression of BFT, is Thomas H. Ogden and Benjamin H. Ogden's (2013) volume entitled *The Analyst's Ear and the Critical Eye: Rethinking Psychoanalysis and Literature*. Finally, by Antonino Ferro (1999), *Psychoanalysis as Literature and Therapy.*

Notes

1 This is not to say that Freud did not make imperishable classic contributions to aesthetics, for example, with his concepts of the uncanny, transience, and sublimation; and with his analysis of jokes (*Witz*) and the *Fort-da* game.
2 Put in a nutshell, the aesthetic conflict is the child's anxious tormenting over the real intentions of an otherness on which it depends in every way. Does the "visible" of the loving, luminous gaze of the mother

express the truth of the "invisible" of the thoughts that are in her head or not? This is simply another way of re-visiting the Kleinian concept of affective ambivalence, while at the same time enriching it with entirely new and personal nuances.

3 See Winnicott (1971, p. 233):

A mother with a baby is constantly introducing and re-introducing the baby's body and psyche to each other, and it can readily be seen that this easy but important task becomes difficult if the baby has an abnormality that makes the mother feel ashamed, guilty, frightened, excited, hopeless. Under such circumstances she can do her best, and no more.

4 See Freud (1926, p. 256): "In psycho-analysis there has existed from the very first an inseparable bond [*Junktim*] between cure and research. ... Our analytic procedure is the only one in which this precious conjunction is assured."

5 "To contain" means to make sense of raw sensorial or emotional experience; there is no "human" sense that is not social.

Chapter 8

Future developments

Intersubjectivity

If I had to say what I think are currently the most relevant and interesting lines of research for BFT, I would indicate the development of a theory of intersubjectivity that helps us to overcome the solipsistic vision of the subject inaugurated by Descartes. I repeat, in my opinion, in psychoanalysis it makes little sense to speak of intersubjectivity simply to mean interaction between separate subjects.

The concept of intersubjectivity has a precise history in philosophy, in particular in Hegel, who does not use this term, but instead talks of recognition, and in Husserl, who is its inventor. In any case, both come to theorize the essentially dialectical and paradoxical nature of our humanity; that is, the fact that the Ego is Ego but also Other, and that only by being Other can it be itself. As I interpret them, we find these key concepts summed up in Bion's concept of *at-one-ment* as the instant when the (singularly emotional or "semiotic") "truth" that promotes the development of the mind arises from the interplay of identity and difference that takes place at moments of emotional unison.

The central idea is that individuals are not isolated entities that then constitute a common field, or vice versa are part of a homogeneous whole that only later differs locally, but are, from the beginning, terms in a dialectical relationship. When in psychoanalysis we stop thinking in terms of dialectics and instead aspire

DOI: 10.4324/9781003219972-8

to an impossible clarity based on dichotomous models, we always get mired in sterile controversies. One of these models based on a binary pair whose terms are separated by a non-transitable caesura is the one that struggles to see the inevitable, and indeed necessary, openness of the subject to the other and to the world.

There is a double narcissistic wound that we have to heal. Not only the awareness that the Ego is not the master in its own house, but that neither is the unconscious. The house of the unconscious is larger than the house in which the individual dwells; it is transindividual or intersubjective. It is this kind of common transcendental area, as Husserl calls it, that can help us intuit how human beings can communicate with each other and empathize, and not the other way round. Or rather, what is shared (instincts and language) and what is distinct (proper body and consciousness) has *always* been presupposed. The difficulty in thinking about this bond of co-implication or co-existence is that the pole of the indistinct is far less visible than the pole of the distinct.

The concepts of subjectivity and intersubjectivity can thus be seen as coinciding with conscious and unconscious, or finite and infinite; on the linguistic plane, with *parole* as the individual embodiment of a sign and *langue* as the social part of language. Could we ever separate the one from the other? Unfortunately, in our models of psychoanalysis we do so all the time, without even noticing. A discipline that claims to rely on its special ability to somehow give shape to and make visible the invisible of the unconscious often fails to avoid being blinded by the light pollution of Descartes' cogito. It seems to think that the solution lies simply in reinforcing the cogito. *But this won't work any more. In physics the last century was that of quantum theories and of the uncertainty principle, and in philosophy, to sum it up with two Merleau-Pontian concepts, that of chiasmus and the flesh* ("chair") *of the world.*

The fact that this has stopped working is evident from the whole history of psychoanalysis. Repeatedly the attempt has been made to expand the territory of the unconscious and consequently to reduce the power of the cogito. We have gone from the pure cognitivism of very early Freud, summarised in the formula of treatment as a translation from the unconscious to the conscious, to postulating the symmetry of the unconscious link and of the analytic field resumed in the Bionian formula of treatment as making unconscious what at first is only conscious. After all, psychoanalysis *per se* has always acted like termites attacking the supporting structures of the house of the Cogito. As we know, Freud did not have a sugarcoated view of the discipline he founded; he talked about his visit to the United States as being like bringing the plague.

I hope that what is at stake is now clear: the philosophical concept of intersubjectivity is useful for refining our theory of the unconscious. The most disingenuous thing there is, but which I suspect is quite widespread, is to think that analysts have a definite and clear concept of the unconscious. *They don't.* The theory, actually a plurality of theories, of psychoanalysis is always evolving. Even a theory is a dynamic field: if one theoretical element changes, all the others change. We can safely assume that we will never come to have a defined and stable concept of the unconscious. By choosing as its polar star a star that cannot be seen, psychoanalysis declares its essence to be positively unstable, non-static, unfulfilled and unfulfillable – just like desire itself.

However, having a more convincing theory of the unconscious is not enough. In fact, it is still necessary to translate it into clinical practice. This implies developing adequate technical tools. We can regard them as such if they regularly give us the opportunity to pass from the visible, obvious, established *I/you* split and to rediscover the *we* – not in order to overthrow the dichotomous and naive setting of our practical realism, but to actually embrace a dialectical vision of the factors that come into play in the process of subjectivation.

This way of conceiving what we call a subject helps us give an answer to another essential question: If the subject is at one and the same time a processuality in which dialectical convergences and divergences between the pole of subjectivity and the pole of intersubjectivity are created, how can we theorize the distinction, which we feel to be indispensable, between *authentic* existence, in which the subject is the master of his own life, and *alienated* existence, in which he is identified with the mass?

Again, the solution is not to think of individuals, groups and masses as entirely distinct entities but as different perspectives on the same entity. What we call an individual can from another point of view (intersubjectivity) be called a group, and what we call a group we can also describe from the point of view of the singularities that constitute it (subjectivity). In my opinion, this means giving up a way of thinking that follows an abstract and divisive logic. If we adopt this view, which can only be defined as dialectical or of mutual exclusion/inclusion, it means that in order to represent the health of the subject we must think not in terms of total and confusing adherence to the group or to its opposite, but rather in terms of the quality of the internal ties that hold the whole together. If the bonds break, the individual falls into the non-consensuality of psychotic thinking. If they stiffen, as when material ties prevail, they lack the elasticity necessary to establish new ties, and this can lead to group psychosis. In either case, the factor that alters the links is *fear*.

Intercorporeity

Linked to the concept of intersubjectivity is that of Intercorporeity. Intercorporeity is the more carnal, physical or non-verbal dimension of intersubjectivity. This is also an area that deserves more systematic exploration than it has received thus far. Winnicott (1955–6) says that the mother's arms are what makes the setting. This proposition should be taken not only metaphorically but also "literally". The setting offers the patient not only psychological but also "material" and sensory support.

Similarly, we should understand Bleger's concept of meta-ego as the deep, "institutional", primitive, non-representational structure of the ego. It makes sense to affirm that analysis is perhaps more a treatment through words that touch than a mere talking cure. We are now all familiar with the pragmatic or performative dimension of words. To speak is to act, and reciprocally to act is also to communicate. If we restrict action as much as possible in analysis, perhaps it is only to simplify an already enormously complex field of observation. But no longer do we invariably think of *acting* as resistance. Action and words are both essential and *inseparable* elements of the dramaturgy of analysis – which is sacred, as it has to do with the social, or rather, divine nature of language and meaning.

References

Aenishanslin J-F (2019). *Les pensées parallèles. Husserl et Freud*. Lausanne: Éditions Antipodes.

Barale F (2008). Postfazione. Griglie e grisaglie. In G Civitarese, *La violenza delle emozioni. Bion e la psicoanalisi postbioniana*. Milan: Raffaello Cortina, pp. 185–198.

Baranger M (2005). Field Theory. In S Lewkowicz & S Flechner, eds., *Truth, Reality and the Psychoanalyst: Latin American Contributions to Psychoanalysis*. London: International Psychoanalytical Association, pp. 49–71.

Baranger M & Baranger W (1961–1962). La situacion analitica como campo dinamico. *Revista Uruguaya de Psicoanálisis* 4(1): 3–5.

Baranger M and Baranger W (1990). *La situazione psicoanalitica come campo bipersonale* (The Psychoanalytic Situation as a Bipersonal Field). Milan: Raffaello Cortina.

Baranger M and Baranger W (2008). The Analytic Situation as a Dynamic Field. *International Journal of Psycho-Analysis* 89: 795–826.

Baranger M and Baranger W (2009). *The Work of Confluence: Listening and Interpreting in the Psychoanalytic Field*. Ed. L. Glocer. London: Routledge.

Bayard P (1999). Is It Possible to Apply Literature to Psychoanalysis? *American Imago*, 56: 207–219.

Bazzi D (2022). Approaches to a Contemporary Field Theory: From Kurt Lewin, George Politzer and José Bleger to Antonino Ferro and Giuseppe Civitarese. *International Journal of Psycho-Analysis* 103: 46–70.

Bezoari M and Ferro A (1989). Listening, Interpretations and Transformative Functions in the Analytical Dialogue. *Rivista di Psicoanalisi* 35 (4): 1012–1050.

Bion WR (1958). On Arrogance. *International Journal of Psycho-Analysis* 39: 144–146. Reprinted in WR Bion, 1967, *Second Thoughts: Selected Papers on Psychoanalysis.* London: Karnac 2007, pp. 86–92.

Bion WR (1959). Attacks on Linking. *International Journal of Psycho-Analysis* 40: 308–315.

Bion WR (1961). *Experiences in Groups and Other Papers.* London: Tavistock.

Bion WR (1962a). *Learning from Experience.* London: Tavistock.

Bion WR (1962b). The Psycho-analytic Study of Thinking. *International Journal of Psycho-Analysisl* 43: 306–310.

Bion WR (1965). *Transformations. Change from Learning to Growth.* London: Maresfield Library, 1991.

Bion WR (1967). *Second Thoughts: Selected Papers on Psychoanalysis.* London: Routledge, 1984.

Bion WR (1992). *Cogitations.* London: Routledge, 2018.

Bion WR and Rickman J (1943). Intra-group Tensions in Therapy–Their Study as the Task of the Group. *The Lancet* 242: 678–681.

Bleger J (1967). Psycho-Analysis of the Psycho-Analytic Frame. *International Journal of Psychoanalysis* 48: 511–519.

Churcher J (2008). Some Notes on the English Translation of *The Analytic Situation as a Dynamic Field* by Willy and Madeleine Baranger. *International Journal of Psychoanalysis* 89: 785–793.

Civitarese G (2008), *The Intimate Room. Theory and Technique of the Analytic Field.* London: Routledge, 2010.

Civitarese G (2013a). *The Necessary Dream.* London: Routledge.

Civitarese G (2013b). Bion's Grid and the Truth Drive. *The Italian Psychoanalytic Annual* 7: 91–114.

Civitarese G (2014). Bion and the Sublime. *International Journal of Psycho-Analysis* 95: 1059–1086.

Civitarese G (2015a). Sense, Sensible, Sense-able: The Bodily but Immaterial Dimension of Psychoanalytic Elements. In H Levine & G Civitarese, eds., *The Bion Tradition.* London: Karnac.

Civitarese G (2015b). Transformations in Hallucinosis and the Receptivity of the Analyst. *International Journal of Psycho-Analysis* 96: 1091–1116.

Civitarese G (2018). *Losing your Head. Abjection, Aesthetic Conflict and Psychoanalytic Criticism.* Lanham: Rowman & Littlefield.

Civitarese G (2019a). The Concept of Time in Bion's "A Theory of Thinking". *International Journal of Psycho-Analysis* 100: 182–205.

Civitarese G (2019b). On Bion's Concepts of Negative Capability and Faith. *The Psychoanalytic Quarterly* 88: 751–783.

Civitarese G (2020a). Regression in the Analytic Field. *Romanian Journal of Psychoanalysis* 13: 17–41.

Civitarese G (2020b). *L'ora della nascita: Psicoanalisi del sublime e arte contemporanea* [The Hour of Birth: Psychoanalysis of the Sublime and Contemporary Art]. Milan: Jaca Book.

Civitarese G (2021a). The Limits of Interpretation: A Reading of Bion's "On Arrogance". International Journal of Psychoanalysis 102(2): 236–257.

Civitarese G (2021b). Bion's Graph of "In Search of Existence". *The American Journal of Psychoanalysis* 81: 326–350.

Civitarese G (2021c). Intersubjectivity and the Analytic Field. *Journal of the American Psychoanalytic Association* 69 (5): 853–893.

Civitarese G (2021d). Experiences in Groups as a Key to "Late" Bion. *International Journal of Psycho-Analysis* 102 (6): 1071–1096.

Civitarese G & Berrini C (2022). On Using Bion's Concepts of Point, Line, and Linking in the Analysis of a 6-year-old Borderline Child. *Psychoanalytic Dialogues*, in press.

Conci M (2011). Bion and his First Analyst, John Rickman (1891–1951): A Revisitation of their Relationship in the Light of Rickman's Personality and Scientific Production and of Bion's Letters to him (1939–1951). *International Forum of Psychoanalysis* 20:68–86.

Eco U (1962). *The Open Work*. Cambridge, MA: Harvard University Press, 1989.

Elliott A & Prager J (2016). *The Routledge Handbook of Psychoanalysis in the Social Sciences and Humanities*. London: Routledge.

Ferro A (1992). *The Bi-Personal Field: Experiences in Child Analysis*. Routledge: London, 1999.

Ferro A (1999). *Psychoanalysis as Literature and Therapy*. London: Routledge, 2006.

Ferro A (2002). *Seeds of Illness, Seeds of Recovery: The Genesis of Suffering and the Role of Psychoanalysis*. London: Routledge, 2005.

Ferro A (2007). *Avoiding Emotions, Living Emotions*. London: Routledge, 2011.

Ferro A, ed. (2013). *Contemporary Bionian Theory and Technique in Psychoanalysis*. London: Routledge, 2018.

Ferro A, ed. (2016). *Psychoanalytic Practice Today: A Post-Bionian Introduction to Psychopathology, Affect and Emotions*. London: Routledge, 2019.

Ferro A et. al. (2007). *Sognare l'analisi*. Turin: Bollati Boringhieri.

Francis St. of Assisi (1998). *The Little Flowers of St. Francis of Assisi*. New York: Random House.

Freud S (1895). *Project for a Scientific Psychology*. In *The Standard Edition of the Complete Psychological Works of Sigmund Freud* 1: 281–391, 1950.

Freud S (1911). Formulations on the Two Principles of Mental Functioning. In *The Standard Edition of the Complete Psychological Works of Sigmund Freud* 12: 213–226, 1950.

Freud S (1916). On Transience. In *The Standard Edition of the Complete Psychological Works of Sigmund Freud* 14: 303–307, 1950.

Freud S (1920). *Beyond the Pleasure Principle.* In *The Standard Edition of the Complete Psychological Works of Sigmund Freud* 18: 65–144, 1950.

Freud S (1921). Group Psychology and the Analysis of the Ego. In *The Standard Edition of the Complete Psychological Works of Sigmund Freud* 18: 1–64, 1950.

Freud S (1926) *The Question of Lay Analysis.* In *The Standard Edition of the Complete Psychological Works of Sigmund Freud* 20: 177–258, 1950.

Freud S (1930). *Civilization and its Discontents.* In *The Standard Edition of the Complete Psychological Works of Sigmund Freud* 21: 57–146, 1950.

Freud S (1932). My Contact with Josef Popper-Lynkeus. In *The Standard Edition of the Complete Psychological Works of Sigmund Freud* 22: 217–224, 1950.

Fuchs T & De Jaegher H (2009). Enactive Intersubjectivity: Participatory Sense-making and Mutual Incorporation. *Phenomenology and the Cognitive Sciences* 8: 465–486.

Fuery K (2018). *Wilfred Bion, Thinking, and Emotional Experience with Moving Images: Being Embedded.* London: Routledge.

Ginzburg C (1986). *Clues, Myths, and the Historical Method.* Baltimore: Johns Hopkins University Press, 2013.

Green A (1998). The Primordial Mind and the Work of the Negative. *International Journal of Psycho-Analysis* 79: 649–665.

Grotstein JS (2004). The seventh Servant: The Implications of a Truth Drive in Bion's Theory of 'O'. *International Journal of Psycho-Analysis* 85: 1081–1101.

Grotstein JS (2007). *A Beam of Intense Darkness: Wilfred Bion's Legacy to Psychoanalysis.* London: Karnac.

Hegel GWH (1807). *The Phenomenology of Spirit.* Cambridge, UK: Cambridge University Press, 2018.

Heidegger M (1987). *Zollikon Seminars. Protocols-Conversations-Letters.* Evanston, IL: Northwestern University Press, 2001.

Kernberg OF (2011). Divergent Contemporary Trends in Psychoanalytic Theory. *Psychoanalytic Review* 98: 633–664.

Klein M (1924). The Role of the School in the Libidinal Development of the Child. *International Journal of Psycho-Analysis* 5: 312–331.

Kristeva J (1980). *Powers of Horror: An Essay on Abjection.* New York: Columbia University Press, 1982.

Kuhn TS (1962). *The Structure of Scientific Revolutions.* Chicago, IL: University of Chicago Press, 1996.

Lacan J (1947). British Psychiatry and the War. *Psychoanalytical Notebooks of the London Circle* 4: 9–34.

Langs R (1976). *The Bipersonal Field.* New York: J. Aronson.

Langs R (1978). *Interventions in the Bipersonal Field.* New York: J. Aronson.

López-Corvo RE (2002). *The Dictionary of the Work of W.R. Bion.* London: Karnac, 2003.

Meltzer D (1984). *Dream-Life: A Re-examination of the Psycho-analytical Theory and Technique.* Strathtay, Scotland: Clunie Press.

Merleau-Ponty M (1945a). The Film and the New Psychology. In *Sense and Non-Sense,* transl. by HL Dreyfus and P Allen Dreyfus, Evanston, IL: Northwestern University Press, pp. 48–59, 1964.

Merleau-Ponty M (1945b). *Phenomenology of Perception.* London: Routledge & Kegan Paul, 2012.

Merleau-Ponty M (1964). *The Visible and the Invisible.* Evanston, IL: Northwestern University Press, 1968.

Neri C, Correale A & Fadda P (1987). *Letture bioniane.* Rome: Borla.

Nissim Momigliano L (1984). Due persone che parlano in una stanza ... (Una ricerca sul dialogo analitico). *Rivista di Psicoanalisi* 30:1–17. Translated as: Two People Talking in a Room: An Investigation on the Psychoanalytic Dialogue. In L Nissim Momigliano & A Robutti, eds., *Shared Experience: The Psychoanalytic Dialogues.* London: Karnac, pp. 5–20, 1992.

Nissim Momigliano L (1992). *Continuity and Change in Psychoanalysis: Letters from Milan.* London: Routledge.

Ogden TH (1989). On the Concept of an Autistic-Contiguous Position. *International Journal of Psycho-Analysis* 70: 127–140.

Ogden TH (2008). Bion's Four Principles of Mental Functioning. *Fort Da* 14: 11–35.

Ogden TH (2009). *Rediscovering Psychoanalysis: Thinking and Dreaming, Learning and Forgetting.* London: Routledge.

Ogden TH & Ogden BH (2013). *The Analyst's Ear and the Critical Eye: Rethinking Psychoanalysis and Literature.* London: Routledge.

Propp V (1928). *Morphology of the Folktale.* Austin: University of Texas Press.

Proust M (1992). *Time Regained. In Search of Lost Time.* Vol. 6. London: Chatto & Windus.

Ricoeur P (1965). *Freud and Philosophy: An Essay on Interpretation.* New Haven, CT: Yale University Press, 1977.

Riolo F (1983) Sogno e teoria della conoscenza in psicoanalisi. *Rivista di Psicoanalisi* 29: 279–229.

Seligman S (2017). *Relationships in Development: Infancy, Inter-subjectivity, and Attachment.* London: Routledge.

Snell R (2020). *Cézanne and the Post-Bionian Field: An Exploration and a Meditation.* London: Routledge.

Spiegelberg H (1972). *Phenomenology in Psychology and Psychiatry: A Historical Introduction.* Evanston, IL: Northwestern University Press.

Vygotskij L & Lurija A (1984). *Strumento e segno nello sviluppo del bambino.* Bari: Laterza, Roma, 1997.

Westen D (1999). The Scientific Status of Unconscious Processes. *Journal of the American Psychoanalytic Association* 47: 1061–1106.

Wilson M (2020). *The Analyst's Desire: The Ethical Foundation of Clinical Practice.* New York: Bloomsbury Academic.

Winnicott DW (1955-6). Clinical Varieties of Transference. In: *Through Paediatrics to Psycho-Analysis.* London: Routledge, pp. 295–299, 2001.

Winnicott DW (1965). *The Maturational Processes and the Facilitating Environment.* London: The Hogarth Press.

Winnicott DW (1971). Basis for Self in Body. In *The Collected Works of D. W. Winnicott,* Vol. 9 (1969–1971). Oxford: Oxford University Press, pp. 225–234, 2017.

Zahavi D (2014). *Self and Other Exploring Subjectivity, Empathy, and Shame.* Oxford: Oxford University Press.

Index